ALICE

A Journey

D1494100

Alice

A Journey

CHRISSY MERTON

Possibility Publishing

First published in 2007
by Possibility Publishing
68 Talfourd Road
London SE15 5NZ
possibilitypublishing@yahoo.co.uk

ISBN 978-09555360-0-7

A CIP record for this book is available from the British Library

Printed by Biddles Ltd
24 Rollesby Road
Hardwick Industrial Estate
King's Lynn
Norfolk PE30 4LS

Note: Some names have been changed in the interest of privacy, but everything else is exactly as I remembered it.

To the memory of my mother
with love and gratitude

Contents

Acknowledgements

Alice was completed with the support of a great many people. My thanks go to Judy Hindley, whose enthusiasm for the first few pages spurred me to continue writing; Melissa Alley, Cynthia de Souza, Nadia Flowers, Roxy Grimshaw, Sally Kendall, Sara Lewandowski, Clare Lewis, Fran Osborne, Nicole Pickford, Debs Rindl, Pepe Salkeld, George Stergiou, Susie Thomson, Isabel Urbanski and Chris Wood, who all read the second draft and gave me very useful constructive criticism; Tania Rice and Emily Buchannan, who used their professional experience to give me some invaluable advice about my style; Imran Shah for his thought-provoking comments on the fifth draft; Noël Janis-Norton for her repeated reading and appreciation of *Alice*; Landmark Education, without which the book would probably have remained as simply a good idea; and above all my husband for tirelessly reading all the drafts and for contributing his extraordinary perceptiveness and loving support.

Thank you also to Renuka Harrison and Robert Smith of Robert Smith Literary Agency, for their appreciation of *Alice* and for procuring me a double-page abridgement in *The Daily Mail*. I am deeply grateful to Sharon Sweeney-Lynch and Becky Gardiner for their meticulous proof-reading and to Marcus Lynch for his generous contribution of the book design.

If I have missed anyone out I am sorry; please feel yourself appreciated anyway.

Grateful acknowledgement is made to the following copyright holders for permission to quote the following extracts:

The C.S.Lewis Company, for *The Magician's Nephew*; Random House, for Peter Matthiessen's *The Snow Leopard*; Stephen Gaskin, for *Mind at Play*; Little Brown, for Dr Verney and John Kelly's *The Secret Life of the Unborn Child*; Landmark Education for the definition of Responsibility. Every effort has been made to trace copyright holders and obtain permission. Any omission brought to our attention will be remedied in future editions.

Prologue

Lying shaking on the scanning table, I was told the baby inside me had a 50-50 chance of survival. I was six months pregnant. Our baby would either live or die, and we had no way of finding out. If my life were a book, I'd flick to the end to see what happened. But I couldn't. I was entering uncharted territory.

In that moment, the future shifted. February 13th 1992 ceased to be the goal ahead of me. I had marked it in my diary with a star as the culmination of nine months and the joyous start of a new life. All my plans for a home birth, dim lights in a peaceful bedroom, dropped away in an instant. The image of a baby, sleeping with its arms above its head, lying between us in bed, the pictures of a toddler exploring our flat, of wheeling a buggy proudly to the shops, of a Christmas spent with the first new addition to our family for 18 years – I didn't dare think of these. The warm security, the cosiness of motherhood, had disappeared. I had lost the certainty of the future, and in its place was an intense experience of the present, moment by moment, that left this time ingrained in my memory.

But that wasn't the beginning of the story. Maybe there never is a beginning, only turning points such as this one, events that alter the future and set you off on a whole new journey.

Chapter One

The Beginning

The year's at the spring,
And day's at the morn.
Morning's at seven,
The hill-side's dew-pearled;
The lark's on the wing;
The snail's on the thorn:
God's in his heaven -
All's right with the world!
Pippa Passes
Robert Browning

June 8th 1991. It is early morning and I am sitting on the edge of the bath and hoping that the plastic stick in my hand will change colour. As I wait, I remember the earlier times, before these plastic sticks were invented, when you had to pee into a little plastic container. Then you shook the pee up in a test tube with mysterious dusty chemicals, and waited for a brown circle to appear in the bottom. You'd see the circle reflected in a mirror at the bottom of the test tube stand. That took twenty minutes. This will only take two. I think of all the bits of carefully made glass and plastic that I have thrown away, disappointed. I remember the thrill of the earlier two occasions when I watched the circle appear, with all the relief of passing an exam, all the excitement of travelling abroad. At last you have the proof in front of you that this time you are actually pregnant. I am nearly 37, have had two miscarriages and spent month after month wondering why on earth I am not getting pregnant again.

The edge of the bath starts to feel hard and cold, so I stand up, still holding the stick level. Yes, it's turning blue. I watch in delight as the shade of blue deepens till it matches the picture on the box. The evidence is indisputable.

I make some tea and get back into bed. It's six-thirty in the morning, and the sky is clear. I can see it, pale blue above the tops of the trees outside the window. Nick is still asleep. Normally I would wake him up to tell him something as exciting as this, but I know now there is plenty of time. I sit and sip my tea, feeling a kind of inner smile spread through my body. It all looked so simple, three years ago, when we first decided to have a baby. Little did I know that I would have two painful miscarriages, and a long wait. When I look back, several years from now, three years will appear so short, so insignificant, but it has seemed interminable. I didn't know it would only be three years. It might have been 10.

I remember my mother pointing out to me that in the Second World War, they had no idea when the war would end. We now know that it lasted six years. But she couldn't think, 'Oh great, it's 1943. Only two more years to go and then we'll have peace.' She had to live with uncertainty day after day, life revolving around air raid sirens, all clears, and the news on the wireless. My mother was teaching in Fort Pitt, Chatham. She told me that every time the air raid warning sounded, the class picked up their gas masks and trooped down to the rooms dug during the Napoleonic War, little windows looking out to sea, high up in the cliffs. She still remembered it clearly, and how they all passed their school certificate, despite the sleepless nights and stressful circumstances. All except Rosie, that is. 'She sat in the back row and hadn't cleaned her teeth since war broke out.' And she told me how you never knew if a bomb would drop on you, or your house. Once, in Chatham, she heard the 'Wheeeeee' of a bomb falling, right overhead, and leaped on a bus as it was moving off. She heard the explosion behind her but didn't turn around. And there was no point in looking ahead to the future. You didn't even know who'd win, let alone when it would all be over. But during these last three years it never occurred to me that I might lose this battle of mine. I trusted I'd have a baby eventually. I just didn't know when. Now I'm on the road, at last.

Nick rolls over beside me and drops an arm across my lap. He is still fast asleep, unaware of his impending fatherhood. The sky above the trees is becoming bluer: a deep, definite shade of blue. My thoughts continue, slowly drifting in this quiet sea of contentment. I've actually been waiting longer than three years. After all, I've always wanted to have children. When I was young I simply assumed I would have them. In my twenties I knew I wanted children one day, but I still wanted to explore life more on my own. Meanwhile, I worked in a children's home and, after university, trained as a teacher; I always enjoyed the company of young people. By the time I reached 30, I remember deciding I was ready. I had discovered the paradoxical freedom, the richness of life that comes from commitment. I wanted to be a mother. I wanted to experience childbirth, to know that strange miracle of producing a new human being and to hold my baby in my arms. I wanted to create a nurturing environment for my child to grow up in, fulfilled, happy and self-reliant. Now it's happening. I feel it is the ultimate act of creation, and some deep part of me, beyond my thoughts or even my feelings, is focused intently upon it. Sitting here, drinking tea, I know all this is still ahead of me. I have simply crossed the divide. I've finally started the journey.

Nick is stirring in his sleep, stretching his legs. He turns on his back and, moving his arm from me, drops it, bent, above his head. His eyes are still shut. I smile at him. He is the most important part of my vision. At 30, I committed myself to finding the right man to share this experience with: someone who would not only be a good father, but my best friend, my lover, my partner in all that we wanted to do. I trusted I would find him. I had no evidence. I simply had my faith in life and my unswerving stand. Within a year of making that commitment we met and, like all good romances, it had been love at first sight. And here he is, five and a half years later, asleep beside me. I glance down to see Nick's blue eyes looking up at me.

'What time is it?' he asks.

'Quarter past seven,' I say, smiling.

'You look happy.'

'I am,' I say, grinning.

There is a pause.

'You're pregnant!'

I nod, grinning from ear to ear.

'How do you know?' he asks, sitting up. 'Have you done the test?'

'Yup!'

There is another pause, while we just look at each other. I can tell he is pleased, slightly excited and mildly confronted. He, like me, seems to just know that this one isn't going to end in a miscarriage. The news is slowly sinking in.

'I'm not old enough to be a father.'

'Don't worry, you never will be old enough.'

It's interesting how we always think that we will reach the 'right time' to have a baby – 'when I've got more money/ a bigger house/ a better car/ finished this job/ feel old enough', till sometimes it's too late. But we're like that about most things in life: we'd rather keep things the way they are till we're fairly certain about the future. And being certain is pretty difficult if you're creating a future that's quite different from the past.

Meeting Nick was an earlier turning point. November 13th 1985. I had talked to him a lot on the phone but had only met him twice. The first time was very brief, but I just had time to think, 'Wow, who is that?!' and take in the wavy fair hair, blue eyes and good looks. The second time he was playing the piano in a concert for The Hunger Project, and I thought, 'That's it. He's the one'. So I phoned him up and asked him to come out to dinner, my heart thumping fast. 'Of course – when?' he said, and I reached for my Filofax.

So there we were, sitting across from each other in The Olive Tree in Leicester Square, Nick with a glass of apple juice and me with a glass of red wine, mentally ticking off our Lists of Ingredients for a Perfect Partner. Mine wasn't actually written out, but I wasn't surprised to find that his favourite country was Nepal (same as mine), and that he'd lived for a while in that beautiful paradise of Asian travelling, Dhulikel Lodge, where I too had stayed (so he liked travelling!); that he was an artist and an architect (perfect); had been at Cambridge University (educated) and had lived in the wilds of Wales (he likes the countryside); that he'd spent two years in the British Virgin Islands, house-sitting and painting (alternative); that he played the piano and was vegetarian. (Ten out of 10!)

He, in turn, noticed that I had travelled around India on my own for eight months, and he had always admired the idea of a woman travelling alone in India; that I was wearing my jumper knitted by a Tibetan woman and bought in Kathmandu; that I played the piano and worked for The Hunger Project, an organisation committed to the end of world hunger; that I had studied English at Oxford. Apparently, this was '9½ out of 10'.

Our conversation went something like this:

Nick: So did you go to India before or after you discovered The Hunger Project?

(She obviously does like me. She hasn't invited me out to ask me to do something for The Hunger Project. I was just being pessimistic.)

Chrissy: (Toying with her aubergine bake) Well, a bit of both really. I was planning to go to India that autumn anyway, and I went to a Hunger Project briefing in the summer that made me think I could actually help in some way.

(He's the Right One all right. And he thinks I'm the Right One, too,

I can tell. He really is gorgeous. I don't feel very hungry.)

Nick: And you went to work at some development project in Gujarat, didn't you?

Chrissy: How did you know?

Nick: Gordon told me. *(That's a nice jumper she's got on. I particularly like that pink bit, and the green matches her eyes.)*

Chrissy: Yes, that's right. Then I set up a charity for them when I came home. *(Gosh, he's been talking about me!)*

Nick: And when did you start working for The Hunger Project? *(Wow, she really is amazing.)*

Chrissy: When I realised that helping on one project wasn't going to make a real difference unless we caused a major shift in the way we, I mean all of us, the world, think and act about hunger. That time in India altered everything for me. I can't forget now that this way of life is only for half the planet. One fifth of us go to bed hungry every night.

(Pause.)

Nick: (looking at Chrissy) There's something not quite right in this conversation. I feel we're not quite being ourselves, or something …

Chrissy: I guess I'm nervous.

Nick: So am I.

(Smile)

⌣

I had decided I was going to meet The One by the end of the year, and so had he. He had even written out his list of What I Would Be Like, including that I would ask him out because he was sick of chasing women. To me he was perfect. He had one last question. He phoned me up a few days later.

'How tall are you?' he asked. I could actually hear the grin on his face.

'Five foot six and a half,' I said. 'Why?'

'Well, I put on my List that you had to be at least five foot six.'

But I'm jumping ahead. As we left The Olive Tree and crossed Leicester Square, we stopped and kissed. At that moment a huge display of fireworks suddenly burst into the sky from the top of the Hippodrome. We looked at each other and smiled. We only worked out later that it was a celebration of Diwali, the Festival of Light, which we had each seen, separately, in Nepal: thousands of little butter lamps burning along garden walls, around temples and along pavements.

That night I took Nick home to meet Cleo. This was important, as she had lived with me for a year or so, and when I got married, Cleo would come too. It was part of the deal. At first, he was a bit jealous. 'You love that cat more than me,' he would say, pretending to sulk, when I sat in bed stroking her long, black-and-white fur while she nuzzled my nose. But soon she would run to greet him when she heard the key in the front door, and gradually he became the one to empty her litter tray. That must be love, I decided.

Eighteen months later we were married, and fulfilled our dream of returning to Nepal together for a month. We stayed in the Himalayan Horizon, the hotel that Nick had designed six years before for B.P.Shresta, the owner of Dhulikel Lodge. We were delighted to find that it had been built in the intervening years by his enormous extended family, using traditional methods. B.P. was most pleased to see us, and let us stay without charge. The food was excellent, and popular with coach parties who came to have lunch on the terrace and watch the long white range of the Himalayas appear above the clouds.

On our return, we decided that now was the time to start a family. I was 33, and it seemed a good idea to have at least my first child before I was 35. I thought, erroneously, that I had plenty of time. But now, at last, I am safely on my way to realising my dream.

That evening I use up the half-drunk bottle of red wine by making black olive and red wine paté and pears in red wine sauce. That's it on alcohol for the next nine months. I also decide to eat lots of salad, have nine hours' sleep every night and an hour's rest during each day. I was told after both my miscarriages that every woman thinks, 'This must be my fault. What did I do wrong?' but about one in five pregnancies ends in miscarriage. But the point is that I did things that I regretted. I worked too hard and didn't rest enough. This time I am going to make sure I have nothing to regret. Fortunately, I'm mainly working with Nick on the administration of his painting classes, so my time is flexible, and I can rest when I need to.

The following weeks are wonderful. At first, there is the sheer relief that the disappointment I felt, each time I had a period, is over. My only symptom seems to be very tender breasts. Then I start to feel slightly travel sick most of the time, which I know is a good sign, as I haven't had this in my previous two pregnancies. It's odd, being glad to feel sick. I get out all the pregnancy books that I bought the first time I was pregnant, and leaf through the well-thumbed pages at the beginning. These show diagrams of how big the embryo/foetus/baby is at each week or month, and explain the symptoms you will be feeling. I get excited when it seems to be more difficult to do up my trousers and the scales register that I've gained a pound.

Eventually I pass the twelve week danger mark and proudly watch my bump grow, still imperceptible to all but me. I stand, naked, in front of the mirror in our bedroom, looking at myself from different angles. I am very slim, (too slim, some people say), so a rounded tummy, normal in most people, is a massive bump in my eyes. Now when I see pregnant women I don't feel sad and envious, I glow with a sense of belonging. I know I am on the other side of the fence at last. And, best of all, I walk into

Mothercare legitimately! Now I'm not looking for something for my niece or nephew, or for a friend's child; I am looking at things for our baby. I wander around, looking at the little dresses and tiny Babygro suits. Passing the highchairs, I see a woman in leggings and a long top who looks ready to give birth any moment. She looks tired but peaceful, and moves slowly. I feel a mixture of excitement and envy: I'm going to look like that one day, but it seems a long way away. I wonder if people can see my bump through my thin summer dress. No, they're all looking at the baby things, living, like me, in their own thoughts and fantasies about the future. It still seems hardly believable that I'm going to have a baby and will need clothes and nappies and baby lotion. I buy a stretchy pregnancy swimsuit, but nothing else. Nine months seems such a long time and, as I can't speed up the arrival of the day I have waited so many years for, I might as well concentrate on the experience of being pregnant, in all its unfolding stages. I will buy baby clothes and nappies when I get to six months.

I talk to Nick about what kind of birth I want. There isn't much need to talk, because we both assume I'll have a home birth; neither of us likes hospitals much and would feel much better at home. Given the question, 'Is it natural for a baby to be born into bright lights and hard clinical surfaces, or to enter the world into a room full of candlelight and soft cushions?' we would have no hesitation in agreeing to the latter. We want to spend time with our baby as soon as it's born, not risk being hurried to clean up. I have read enough to know that home births are statistically safer, and you have less chance of unnecessary medical interference. I know that the important thing is to feel in charge of this intensely powerful experience, and that to give birth on my own territory is clearly more likely to put me at ease than being in hospital. My limited experience of hospitals has left me with lasting associations of fear, discomfort and a feeling of helplessness.

It's ironic that when my mother had my sister in Leeds in 1948, she said she had to fight to get a hospital birth, because most people still had their babies at home. Her mother, my grandmother, had her at home, with a doctor in attendance, as was the norm in 1917. (He, incidentally, decided things weren't moving fast enough and used forceps. My grandmother made sure she only had a midwife when she had her second child.)

I read a lot, to arm myself with knowledge. What about my age? Well, apart from the statistical increase in chromosomal abnormalities, problems in pregnancy and childbirth do not increase in proportion to age. Increased problems are correlated to ill-health, lack of fitness, obesity and smoking. I am healthy fit, slim and have never smoked.

The only question we wonder about is whether to have community midwives, who are on the NHS, or independent ones, who you have to pay. I know friends who have had both. One friend who booked with a team of NHS community midwives, said she didn't know which one would actually deliver the baby. Where that left her was really hoping that one particular midwife wouldn't deliver it, because she found her rather harsh and bossy. We decide on independent midwives so we can all get to know each other and I won't have that worry about who is delivering our baby.

So, at three months, I book a pair of independent midwives who have been recommended to me, and they arrange to come and see us. It is exciting ringing them up. I mean, it's not something that anyone can do, like ringing up a plumber, or a financial advisor, or a piano teacher. I know it sounds obvious, but you have to be pregnant. So? What's the big deal? Of course you have to be pregnant. But in that moment, in something as mundane as making a phone call, I experience the wonder of crossing that invisible border into a new dimension, and the strangeness of a timeline that is independent of our minds. It's a bit like waking up to find that you've turned into a garden, or a greenhouse.

'You really are pregnant, aren't you?' says Nick.

We take an immediate liking to Nicky and Katrina. They aren't dressed in a blue uniform and don't carry black bags, and they fit my picture of alternative midwives. They are solid, warm, and slightly eccentric. Nicky has shortish brown hair and wears a grey track suit. She has three grown-up children, used to be married to a goat farmer and has written several books on childbirth and childcare. She is the organiser: clear about a woman's right to plan what she wants for pregnancy and childbirth; firm, decisive and sympathetic. A good person to have on our side, I decide; little realizing just how valuable these qualities are going to be. Katrina is Australian, and has short black hair that stands on end on top of her head. Later, I will see her after she has been wearing a woolly hat, and her hair is flat. She looks completely different. She seems kind and gentle. She works as Nicky's midwifery partner, but is actually a doctor and part-time GP. They have an air of motherly care, but also of being real partners. There is no 'them and us' about them, no 'we know, you don't', which I have often experienced in hospitals. This is our team.

We sit around the dining room table eating fasolada with crusty brown bread. Fasolada is a soup made with lots of olive oil, onions, garlic, black-eyed beans, tomatoe purée, stock and lemon-juice, cooked and whizzed in a blender. It is delicious, and I will always associate it with that first lunch, with the red tablecloth and the summer breeze blowing the curtains gently through the open window.

Soon I start going round to Nicky and Katrina's house for antenatal visits. It is always fun visiting them. As Nicky is busy doing an advanced midwifery course, I see more of Katrina in the early months. I am always ready for a pee by the time I arrive, so she hands me one of those cardboard sticks on the way up to the loo; they measure the glucose and protein levels in your urine. Mine are always normal. As I drink a pint mug of tea, sitting on a comfy sofa with piles of assorted cushions, we chat away about Nick's work, what it feels like to be pregnant, what other people think about home births, where we went for the weekend and so on. She takes my blood pressure and sometimes takes a blood sample, which she luckily never warns me about, so I don't have to dread it on the bus on the way here. I never watch when I have a needle stuck in my arm, not since, at the age of six, I fainted after watching Doctor Crawshaw give me a typhoid vaccination. Katrina gives me a beautifully painted little papier-mâché egg to hold, to make the vein stand out. We keep chatting away as I stare at the goldfish, the trailing plants, or the bookshelves packed with interesting books on childbirth, and try to be relaxed about the needle going into my arm. I hate needles.

Katrina has a little daughter, Molly, who is about three, lively and fun, with straight black hair and bright eyes. Sometimes Molly comes in, and bounces on the piles of scatter cushions. She pretends to be the doctor, and Katrina shows her how to feel my tummy and listen with a stethoscope. Soon Katrina is listening to the baby's heartbeat, and to my delight 'plays' it to me with a little ultrasonic device held against my abdomen. I will always remember the first time I hear that fast little drumming sound, and finally experience I am not alone. There are two of us. I rush home to tell Nick about it.

What a wonderful summer! It seems to be sunny all the time. We create a project to increase our income, writing a list of 13 possible ways, including Nick busking with a portable electric piano. We have decided to go for doing commissions of black-and-white portraits. We sit down by the phone with a list of our friends and acquaintances. Nick looks decidedly uncomfortable.

'What are your concerns?' I ask.

'Well, I think they'll feel obliged to say yes.' Pause.

'OK. What else?'

'I'm not a good enough artist; it's a cheek to ask them.'

I smile. 'What else?'

'They will say no. I'll be embarrassed.'

'OK. What else?'

He looks at me. 'I can't think of anything else.'

'Now pick up the phone and dial!' I say.

Of course all his fears disappear as soon as he is in conversation with people, and he is amazed that most people say yes, and are delighted to be given the opportunity. They are very pleased with their portraits, which they keep for themselves or give to their grandmothers for Christmas. We get one commission in a most unusual way. A woman phones us who works as a waitress. She served a couple in a restaurant who had a portrait of themselves leaning against the wall. They were taking home the one Nick had done of them. Can she have one done of her daughter, she asks?

I do various office jobs, always somehow managing to work the hours I like: afternoon and evening. I also start to get very un-vegetarian cravings for sausages and bacon, which I indulge in (much to Cleo's delight) and put on some much-needed weight.

⁓

I do what every woman I know does when pregnant. Between the antenatal visits, work and salads, I read books, day-dream, visit friends with babies and become very emotional watching television programmes about suffering children.

As well as reading my old pregnancy and childbirth books, I find two new ones. The first is *Three in a Bed* by Deborah Jackson. Ever since our trips to Nepal and India, Nick and I have each felt that it makes perfect sense to have your baby sleeping in bed with you, as they do in these countries, rather than putting him or her in a separate cot, in a different room. We very rarely saw babies or children crying in either country, and I saw how much confidence and self-assurance they had. Sleeping with their parents, we felt, was an important factor. So there is no need to buy a cot, and the Moses basket Nick's parents gave us the first time I became pregnant will do for the baby's daytime sleeps. Then he or she can be in the same room as me whatever I am doing.

The other book that I read is *The Secret Life of the Unborn Child* by Dr Thomas Verny and John Kelly. It appeals to my sense of the magical, mystical nature of pregnancy. The writer describes how he stays with some friends in the country, and often finds Helen, seven months pregnant, singing a lullaby alone to her unborn baby. After his birth, this song seems to have a magical effect on him. No matter how upset he is, this song will always quieten him down.

'I already knew,' Dr Verny writes, *'that at one time or another every expectant mother senses that she and her unborn child are reacting to one another's feelings.'*

I muse on how subtle and powerful are the instincts which we, in our Western, 'civilised' culture have, to a large extent, suppressed. I can't wait to get to five months, so that I can start singing to the baby inside me.

I also find myself watching Nick Danziger's video diary on television, about his trip to Afghanistan. A little girl screaming in hospital after stepping on a mine on the way to the bread shop, a little boy who thinks all his family have been destroyed by a bomb, leave me weeping in anguish, and Danziger's building of a children's home to save the orphans currently housed in a lunatic asylum has me moved to tears by his love and commitment. I feel a bit like an emotional limp rag for a few hours afterwards, unable to eat anything.

Watching that video makes me very aware of the extremes of this world. I can be sitting in total safety, comfort and comparative luxury, reading books about what happens to babies in the womb and different options for birth and pain relief, or thinking about whether to buy a cot for the baby or not, while mothers in other parts of the world are seeing their children killed, watching them die of diarrhoea, or having to choose between giving them polluted water to drink or letting them die of thirst.

Vivid pictures come to my mind of my time at Amari Mandali, the project for tribal women that I visited in Gujarat, when I was travelling in India. I remember the story Mira, the organiser, told me about finding a woman on the road, carrying her 16-year-old daughter on her back, trying to hitch a lift from a lorry to a hospital. The girl was dying of anaemia, and Mira could see from looking at her that she was past saving. She was thin and pale, and had no energy left, but the mother was crying, desperate to get her to the hospital. The girl was dead by the time a lorry came by.

But despite poverty and widespread illiteracy, generally the people in the villages were so happy. The 12-year-old girls training in the carpet-weaving co-operative were constantly laughing and singing, bubbling over with a natural joy in life. In contrast, I remember Vanita, dressing up in her best clothes and putting on a brave face for the camera. But she couldn't hide her careworn, sad look. She had been unable to have any children, so her husband, who also looked pretty unhappy when I saw him, had had to marry again. It was vital to have children to look after you in your old age. He spent most of his time with his new wife and child, and Vanita was left to look after the house and work in the fields. She was lonely and unfulfilled.

I think of Nick in the next room, painting; I stroke my rounded belly and give silent thanks for my good fortune.

We both feel we have been let into a new world. Now we can talk about babies and children with our friends from a new standpoint. We are beginning to enter the land of the initiated. Conversations that are commonplace for our friends Sara and Peter are like Christmas presents for us. One Sunday morning, for example, they come round to drop off a baby bath for us about eleven o'clock. We are dressed, but still eating breakfast.

'It's all right for some, isn't it?' remarks Sara, as she flops down on the sofa. 'Guess what time we got woken up – five o'clock! The sun was shining. Now he's tired himself out.'

I look at Emil, asleep in his buggy, and Sara's large tummy.

'Wait till there's two of them in your bed,' I say.

'That won't be for another two months, but I'm getting a bit fed up. I want it all over now. I'd rather be kicked on the outside than the inside.'

'Thank God for the king-sized bed,' Peter says. They bought it in Thailand. It's enormous; it must be at least seven feet wide. 'But Emil's started to work his way round in his sleep. He ends up across the bed, with his feet in my mouth.'

'Nick's looking worried,' comments Sara. 'You don't want to change your mind do you?'

'No, I'm not worried,' says Nick.

'It's just that inscrutable look again,' Sara says. 'I never really know what you're thinking.'

'Not much. I was just listening, and eating my muesli.'

'And translating into Martian,' I add.

I should explain at this point that Nick is actually from Mars. He has long artistic fingers that look as if they have suckers on the ends, and quite often you can tell he is having to translate the question into Martian in order to understand it.

Nick scrapes out the last bits of cereal and moves towards the sink. There is a single clear 'Mew!' from by his leg, so he reaches down and puts the bowl on the floor.

'Sorry, Cleo. I nearly forgot.'

'What's the Secret of Getting the Cereal Bowl?' I ask.

'Timing,' says Nick.

'What is this?' asks Peter. 'You two are always going on about "Timing".'

'Oh, we've got this old Rowan Atkinson tape,' I tell him. 'It goes – Ready Nick? – I say, I say, I say; what's the secret of good comedy?'

'I don't know,' says Nick. 'What is the – '

'Timing.'

Sara laughs. 'I don't get it,' Peter says.

'Oh, stop it, Peter,' says Sara. 'Go and make us some coffee.'

'These two probably haven't got any. They drink dandelion roots and bats' milk.'

'Actually we have got some,' I reply. 'We keep it for visitors and other stray coffee addicts. Anyway, I like the smell.'

There is a thumping noise as Cleo charges up the hall passage, jumps on a chair, and hurtles back, ears flat, eyes bright.

'Well, I hope your baby isn't as eccentric as your cat,' says Sara. 'Though, actually, it might be quite interesting.' We all look at Cleo, images passing through our minds of a baby with pointy black ears racing at 20 miles an hour on all fours along the passage.

Katrina offers me the Bart's Triple Test, and I decide to have it. It's a simple blood test, from which you are given a probability of your baby having Down's syndrome. There's no risk of miscarriage, as the needle is stuck in your arm, not your uterus, as with an amniocentesis. Also, I decide, it will be a lot less painful. Just looking at the photo of an amniocentesis is too uncomfortable for me – I avoid page 52 of Miriam Stoppard's *Pregnancy and Birth Handbook*.

On September 4th the results of the Bart's Test come back – 1 in 900! I am very glad I've done it. Now I can relax, with no worries at the back of my mind.

Summer changes to autumn; the trees in the park outside our window turn yellow and red, and soon wet leaves cover the pavements. As I grow heavier and slow down, I muse on the 'Season of mists and mellow fruitfulness', and the ripening child in my belly. 'We do admire the way you are growing this baby,' Nicky and Katrina often say. I love the idea that I am actively growing my own little human being.

At four and a half months I write 'Half-way' in my diary in pencil. My tummy is now round, and my navel has undone itself. It is fascinating. A brown line appears, running vertically down over the bump and through my inverted navel. Lying in the bath it looks like a path going up a hill.

Soon I begin to feel the baby moving inside me. They aren't kicks, as I've heard people describe, just butterfly movements, like a little fish. Sometimes I lie in the bath and watch my bump change shape as the baby moves around. It is a perpetually exciting experience, watching my body grow, noticing my moods, feeling the new life growing inside me.

I am euphorically happy. My life is perfect.

Chapter Two

Turning Points

In terms of game theory, we might say the universe is so constituted as to maximise the play. The best games are not those in which all goes smoothly and steadily towards a certain conclusion, but those in which the outcome is always in doubt. Similarly, the geometry of life is designed to keep us at the point of maximum tension between certainty and uncertainty, order and chaos.

Every important call is a close one. We survive and evolve by the skin of our teeth. We really wouldn't want it any other way.

The Silent Pulse
George Leonard

I am just making myself some dandelion coffee after lunch when the phone rings.

'Chrissy, it's started. It'll probably go on for hours yet, but – excuse me a moment...' It is Sara's voice, sounding rather breathless. She turns away from the phone and I can hear her panting heavily, like someone running uphill carrying bricks. I am intrigued. I've never heard anyone in labour before, only people acting in films. After about a minute she is back.

'Sorry about that. I just have to keep stopping. Can you come round? It's just that Peter's at work and there's no one to look after Emil.'

'Sure, I'll get a taxi. Nick's out. I should be there in half an hour.'

As I rush downstairs to get in the taxi, I feel excited, being part of this female-pregnancy-childbirth world. Here I am, five months pregnant, helping my friend go through her labour. I belong to this world now.

Like me, Sara has booked to have a home birth with two independent midwives, and has been incredibly efficient about organising a support team to be called on when the labour starts. She has a list of all the dates we are available, and has even had us around for a briefing meeting. 'Your main job will be to look after Emil, give him food, change his nappies, but also to take care of Peter and the midwives, getting them food, making drinks, maybe going to the corner shop. But I'll make sure there's plenty of food in the flat. And if it's in the middle of the night, bring night-clothes, and you and Nick can sleep in the bed with Emil till he wakes. We'll be in the study. I've set it up with a birthing pool and cushions...'

Well, neither Peter nor Nick will be there for a while. I wonder how like her plans this is going to be. I ring the doorbell and can hear the pants and groans as Sara comes along the corridor. The door opens and there she is, doubled over and walking slowly.

'Hi, thanks for coming.'

'That's all right. Have you phoned the midwives yet?' I make sure my voice sounds calm, as if I am used to my friends having contractions while we are talking.

'Yes, I called Becky, but I told her it would be several hours yet,' she says dismissively. 'This is just how it was with Emil, and he took ages.'

She kneels on the sofa and leans on the arm, breathing heavily as another contraction comes over her. I time it. It is strange, to know that she is here, and can hear me, but also not here, taken over by what is going on in her body. Maybe she can't hear me. I rub her back awkwardly, wondering what I am meant to do or how I am meant to be. The two cats are slinking about, watching her dubiously, and Emil is holding on to the side of her trousers. I haven't spent much time with children of 20 months, and feel rather inept.

'It's all right, Emil,' Sara says in a completely normal voice as soon as she can speak. I envy her, as I have so many times before, for having that special relationship mothers have with their own children. I can't wait.

'Chrissy, could you put those notes through the door of the houses on either side?' she asks me, handing me a pile of cards. I read them as I go outside. 'The home-birth in no. 23 has started. There may be some noise for a while. Thank you for your support.'

There is a lot of noise outside as well, as it is November 5th, and the darkening sky is intermittently bursting with colour. I return to find Sara having another contraction. I have visions of her giving birth all over the sitting room floor, with nothing to protect the carpet, and, worse than that, the cord round the baby's neck or something. I decide it is time to take matters into my own hands and get on the phone. The conversation is short and to the point.

'Becky, it's Chrissy, I'm at Sara's. Yes, they're happening every minute. OK, see you soon.'

I am glad to know she is coming straight away. I can see Sara is much further into the labour than she realises. I wait for half an hour, playing with Emil, talking to Sara when I can, and listening in wonder to the moans and heavy breathing that I have never knowingly heard before but which sounded so natural and so distinct, somehow, from other human sounds. I feel I recognise them, perhaps from my own birth? I notice how completely dependent on other people's help you are in childbirth, too; it just takes over, and everything else has to line up with it. Considering how organised my life has been for a long time, I find it exciting to be involved with something that is completely out of my hands, without it being something bad, like an accident or an illness.

The doorbell rings and I open it to a woman in her thirties, carrying a big black bag. She smiles, tells me she is Becky, and asks where Sara is. I am relieved, because here is someone who knows what to do, and Emil is becoming increasingly fretful. She manages to be appreciative of my presence, encouraging to Sara and gently in charge. I take Emil down to the bedroom and we play a game hiding his slippers in the bed. He only stops once or twice to wonder what his mother is doing in the sitting room, but the game is interesting enough to occupy his attention. I am bored, but have to appear completely engrossed in the game. This would have been Peter's job if he had been home from work, but he isn't. Sara phoned him when the labour started and told him it would be hours yet, and he didn't need to come home early. He'll miss the birth now, I reckon. I don't think I could bear to give birth without Nick there, but I suppose this isn't her first baby. Maybe it's different. This thought reminds me of the conversation Nick and I had last night, and I smile to myself.

I was getting increasingly impatient with having to do most of the shopping, cooking and housework over the last couple of weeks, as well as going out to work. It wasn't that Nick didn't help when he was there, but he was out a lot. And he wasn't even earning money. He had agreed to do some volunteer work for a week, and it had somehow become two weeks. I had come home the night before, carrying some rather heavy shopping after a long day at work, to find the washing up not done and the bedroom a mess. Then I looked outside the back door and saw the maggots. We had tried a special cat litter made of non-porous granules – coated maize or something – and the idea was the cat peed through them and on to newspaper. All you had to do was change the newspaper and 'dispose of the solid matter' with a special scoop – good for the environment and all that. It was meant to be odour-free, but after several weeks we felt the grains needed rinsing. Nick had put them in a bucket of water, but never got around to drying them out, and here was the bucket of grains, crawling with maggots. I shut the back door with gritted teeth and found a pen and an A4 pad. I wrote a furious letter full of capitals and triple underlinings, stating just how fed up I was and making clear, numbered requests – well, I suppose they were demands – about sharing the work. I left it lying in the middle of the hall floor, made myself some supper, then went to bed.

About eleven o'clock I woke up to hear the key turn quietly in the lock and Nick open the door. There was a pause while he read the letter. I wasn't nearly so annoyed after writing it, but I wasn't exactly pleased, either. He came down the hall and into the bedroom, carrying the letter.

'Wow, you really expressed yourself,' he said.

'You're not meant to say that!' I said crossly. 'You're meant to say, "You're right, I'm a horrible scumbag." '

'You're right, I'm a horrible scumbag,' said Nick.

'Well, what are you going to do about it?!'

'I'm going to do the shopping from now on, and I'm going to sit down with you tomorrow afternoon and we'll look at the income plan.'

'What about the cat grains?'

'I'll clean them up. Tomorrow morning.'

'And I won't have to remind you?' I asked, suspiciously.

'You won't have to remind me.'

There was a pause. Nick was smiling, but I continued to frown, despite the temptation to smile back.

'Well, that's no good,' I said. 'I want to be annoyed with you for longer.' Now I couldn't help smiling. 'OK, get me an Ovaltine and I'll forgive you.'

Sitting here with Emil, in someone else's bedroom, I miss Nick, and want to be at home. I wonder how long we'll be here. I can't get to the kitchen for a drink because it means going through the sitting room. Then, only an hour and a quarter after Becky arrives, I suddenly hear a new voice, the cry of a baby that isn't Emil. I somehow forgot that that is what happens, even though it is always like that in Victorian novels or early films. But there's nothing clichéd about the experience. I am full of anticipation when Lucyanne, the other midwife who arrived just before the birth, calls Emil and me down to the sitting-room. 'It's a little girl,' she says, smiling.

We enter softly, aware of the newness of every sound and sight to the little being fresh into the world. The electric fire glows brightly in the subdued light, and the room feels very warm and cosy after coming through the cold hall. Sara is sitting naked on a towel on the sofa, with her little daughter in her arms, lying on a small electric blanket. She is talking gently to her, and the baby is gazing steadily into her eyes. I am moved with wonder at how overwhelming the sense of newness is, that there is nothing going on with this little human being; she is just there, gazing. Sara looks up. She is bright-eyed and there is sweat in her hair; she looks as if she has just run several miles and there is a sense of peace and accomplishment on her face.

This is a real home birth. This is how mine is going to be.

⌣

It is soon after I am six months pregnant, in early November, that I start to notice a strange pain under my ribs.

'Nicky, it's Chrissy. I've got this strange pain, kind of north-west of my stomach. It's been there about three days. Katrina said when she saw me that it was just that I'm getting bigger, but it doesn't feel like it.'

'Is it worse just after you've eaten?'

'No, it's just there all the time. It hurts more when I press it.'

'Well, it's probably just your muscles expanding, but it could be your gall bladder. If it doesn't get better tomorrow, I'd go and see your GP.'

I am not due for another antenatal visit for over two weeks, and Nicky doesn't sound concerned about it. But I am in pain, so I decide I will go to the doctor.

⌣

The next day, at four o'clock, I am sitting in the waiting room at my local clinic, reading the posters about 'What to do if you have flu',

'Have you had your child vaccinated yet?', 'Repeat Prescriptions', and looking at the neglected plants in the little square courtyard. There isn't much to recommend the Sixties 'little boxes' design of the building, but at least the chairs are comfortable and padded, which I appreciate. Perhaps the NHS can't run to a gardener. There are a lot of other people waiting, mainly old people and young mothers with small children. I have only been here once before, a long time ago. I don't feel at home here. The worrying thing about having a system with no advance appointments is that every time a doctor calls a name incoherently into his microphone you sit alert in case he called your name and you didn't recognise it. You are only sure it wasn't you when someone else stands up and walks down the corridor.

The doctor looks up when I come in, which I think is promising. I tell him about the pain.

'Sounds like your gall bladder,' he says, 'but let's have a look.'

I lie on the couch and he presses the area round my stomach.

'Well, I can't be sure. I'll send you up to the hospital for an ultrasound scan, but meanwhile cut out all fat.'

He hands me a pink form with a phone number on and tells me to make an appointment.

'And if it is my gall bladder, what can I do?'

'Nothing really, just cut out fat and it should get better eventually.'

I go home and look up 'gall bladder' in Adelle Davis's Let's Eat Right to Keep Fit. It says: 'A certain amount of fat is necessary to stimulate the production of bile and the fat-digesting enzyme, lipase. Only when fat enters the intestine does the gall bladder empty itself vigorously. Without fats, too little bile is formed, and the gall bladder holds its reserve bile. This faulty emptying may be contributing to the formation of gall stones. If a fat-free diet is continued for long, the gall bladder eventually shrivels or atrophies. Yet vitamins A, D, E and K, as they occur naturally, cannot be absorbed from the intestines into the blood without the presence of fat and bile. Deficiencies of these vitamins can be caused either by fat-free diets or by bile failing to reach the intestine.'

I get a large bowl of lettuce, pour French dressing over it and eat it.

⌣

'Hello, this is the Ultrasound Department,' says a weary voice.

'Hello,' I reply. 'I've got a form here to book for an ultrasound scan. I'm pregnant and I've got a pain under my ribs. My doctor thinks it may be my gall bladder.'

'You're pregnant? Oh, they've put you through to the wrong department. Hold on a moment.'

I hold on.

'Hello, Obstetric Ultrasound.'

'Hello, I'm 27 weeks pregnant and I need to have a scan for my gall bladder.'

'Sorry, I don't understand. Have you been here before?'

'No.'

'And you're 27 weeks pregnant?' She sounds rather shocked.

'Yes.'

'Didn't antenatal send you up here at 20 weeks?'

'I haven't been to antenatal. I've got independent midwives. My doctor wants me to have a scan because I've got a pain under my ribs.'

'Is it the baby kicking you?'

'No, it's higher up than my uterus. He thinks it might be my gall bladder, but I don't think it is.'

'Well I'm afraid we only scan the baby here; you need the ordinary Ultrasound Department. I'll transfer you.'

'Hello, Ultrasound Department.'

'Hello, I called just now. It is you I wanted. Can I make an appointment to have my gall bladder scanned?'

'Certainly; I'll just look in the book.'

Sound of pages flicking.

'Right, the first one's January 24th,' she says calmly.

'January 24th! That's 10 weeks! But, but – I'm in pain!'

'Well that's the first we've got. I'm sorry, dear.'

I will either have died or given birth by then.

'Well, could you call me if you get a cancellation?' I ask, as a last attempt.

'That was a fat lot of good!' I say to Nick, as I put the phone down. 'I don't think it's my gall bladder anyway, but what if it had been...?'

Each day the pain is slightly worse. It starts to make me constantly uncomfortable. By Friday I feel unable to go to my Active Birth class, and call my teacher. She is most sympathetic, and recommends I try Jeremy Gilbey, a very good cranial osteopath. He will probably be able to tell me what is causing the pain and maybe he can ease it, if it is simply created by expanding muscles. I know from previous experience with back pain what an extraordinary ability osteopaths have to diagnose what is going on in your body from touch and from looking carefully at your spine. So, as western medicine seems to have failed me, I'll try alternative medicine. I call and make an appointment for Tuesday.

All I have to do is sit on a 36 bus till I reach Bayswater, but it isn't an easy journey. It is a long way from Camberwell, and it is a grey, drizzly day. The pain under my ribs seems to dominate everything else, and I am so relieved when I can finally get off and walk slowly up the street. I press the buzzer and a friendly voice says, 'Hello, Chrissy, come on in'. I push the front door open and find myself in a long passage lined with blue and white Victorian tiles. A staircase at the end leads to the consulting room on the first floor. A head appears over the edge of the banisters.

'Hello, Chrissy. I'll be finished very soon, if you'd like to take a seat in the waiting room.'

I feel welcomed and at home. The waiting room consists of three elegant dining-room chairs in a little corridor with pictures on the wall and a coffee table piled with *House and Garden* magazines. If only NHS clinics could create the same atmosphere. Maybe some do. Maybe I've always lived in the wrong places. I browse through the copies of *House and Garden*, luring me into coveting a large, beautiful house in the country.

It isn't long before Jeremy says goodbye to the previous patient and ushers me into a beautiful square room. There is an osteopathic couch in the middle, like a long, high table with a towelling-covered top. White muslin curtains hang at the two long Regency windows, the walls are painted deep blue and hung with antique Japanese paintings. He sits at a little bureau while he takes a thorough medical history of myself and my family, and I check out a bookcase containing intriguing books on anatomy. It reminds me of the cave-house belonging to Mr Tumnus, the faun, in *The Lion, the Witch and the Wardrobe*. Tumnus has a shelf of books with titles such as *The Life and Letters of Silenus*, *Nymphs and Their Ways*, and *Is Man a Myth?*.

After looking carefully at my back, he asks me to lie on the couch and works on my head and sacrum, at the base of my spine, making very tiny, almost imperceptible movements. He explains what he is doing, helping the body to realign itself and helping lymphatic drainage. This much I do understand, but some of what he says is beyond me, as remote as computer programming or Tibetan. His knowledge of anatomy is amazing, and he clearly knows what he is doing. It's so nice to relax on a couch for half an hour and have healing hands on me. He says I should feel better within three days, and makes an appointment for me to come again in a week.

I feel slightly better for a day or two, but then the pain increases, till my whole abdomen seems to ache. Walking and sitting down are worst. The only position I am comfortable in is lying on my side, but I have to keep changing sides to avoid getting sciatica.

Cleo, of course, thinks this is for her benefit. She settles down on the bed next to my bump, and then, when I turn over, just snuggles into my back. At night I sleep fitfully, constantly woken by sciatica.

When I look back, it will seem strange that I don't phone Nicky or Katrina again. Why doesn't it occur to me that there might be something going on outside my knowledge? I probably don't want to admit to myself that I can't handle it. I want the pain just to go away, for it to be a phase of the pregnancy I am going through, for there to be something wrong with me, not the baby.

Nick is wonderful. He calmly does all the cooking, washing up and shopping as well as working, and comforting me when I feel worried by the pain. I think he is more concerned than he lets on, but he trusts me to do what I feel is right. I feel so taken care of.

We have booked to go to a John Lill piano recital at the Royal Festival Hall on the afternoon of Sunday December 1st. It is 18 days after the pain first appeared. I am noting it all carefully in my diary. I decide to go, but sitting down in the first half is as much as I can bear, so I spend the second half wandering slowly around the foyers and shops, strains of Schumann's *Carnaval* in the distance.

The next day I am due to go to Katrina's, but I phone up that morning in desperation, asking her to come to me. I can't face another bus ride.

'You don't look very well, do you?' she says, looking concerned but relaxed. I realise when she arrives how reassured I feel that she is here, how much anxiety I've suppressed, surviving day by day through the last couple of weeks. She gets out her tape measure and measures the distance over Glastonbury Tor.

'I can see why you've been in pain,' she says. 'Your tummy's grown too fast. It's 36cm. It should only be about 30cm. You shouldn't be this size for another 8 weeks. I'll make an appointment for you to get scanned at King's.'

She fetches the phone. Despite her calmness, I feel uneasy, and ask, 'Why does it happen?'

'It means that the baby isn't swallowing enough. You see, babies swallow amniotic fluid and pee it out. It goes round in this cycle. But if a baby goes on peeing out and doesn't swallow enough, you have too much amniotic fluid.'

She has got through to the Obstetric Ultrasound Department. 'Hello, it's Dr Allen here. Can I make an appointment for one of my patients to have a scan? She's 30 weeks and has polyhydramnios. Nothing till Wednesday?' She pauses a moment. 'Well, OK.'

'So where does it come from?' I am thinking this through slowly.

'From you, through the placenta and down the umbilical cord.'

'I thought I was drinking quite a lot recently. So why do you think the baby isn't swallowing?'

'I don't know, it could be a number of things; it could be something minor.'

'What did you say it was called? Hydr....?'

'Polyhydramnios.'

'Oh yes. Much water.'

I separate the word into its parts, matter-of-factly, learning this new language for my baby, for our joint lives. My mind wants to understand it, how it works, like a child taking apart a jigsaw and putting it back together again.

<hr>

The appointment is for twelve noon on Wednesday December 4th, two days away. Somehow I drag myself through those two days. I go to see Jeremy Gilbey on the Tuesday. I take a taxi there, which is slightly better than the bus, though every bit of rough tarmac seems to jar through me. Jeremy listens sympathetically to what I tell him, and says he can see that my abdomen has grown a lot just in a week. He says he can help to ease the sciatica a bit, and help my lymphatic drainage. I tell him I've noticed already that despite my increased weight the oedema in my right ankle has completely gone. I no longer look as if my lower right leg has been borrowed from a small elephant. My ankle-bones have reappeared.

I take the bus back because, I think, at least I can stand up. But so many kind people, thinking from the size of my tummy and my tired face that I am about to give birth any moment, keep offering me their seats, and in the end I haven't the strength to resist. I sit down and endure the long journey home. That evening two friends who were on the staff of The Hunger Project with me, Isabel and Dan, stay to supper. Nick has drawn their portraits. Isabel sympathetically rubs my back, but the only thing that gives me any relief is putting the cold tub of ice-cream on the top of my bump. That works till we eat the ice-cream.

Chapter Three

The Long Day

Make your choice, adventurous stranger,
Strike the bell and bide the danger;
Or wonder, till it drive you mad,
What would have followed if you had.
                    The Magician's Nephew
                    C S Lewis

It is the morning of December 4th. This is the day. I have no idea what is going to happen, and I don't let myself imagine anything. I know any imaginings will only get me pointlessly worried and won't help. Basically, I don't like hospitals. They mean needles, drugs and operations and a fear that things are out of my control. Long waits in dilapidated corridors and young doctors working ridiculously long hours. I don't even remind myself that I don't like hospitals. I have to go there and that is that.

'Darling, can you help me put my boots on?'

For a week or so now, I have been unable to reach my feet, and my boots are the only pair of shoes I can still get into. Nick is kneeling on the floor pulling on my ankle boots and tying the laces.

'This is good practice for having children, you realise,' I tell him.

'Yes, I suppose so. So, are you all right, Sweetheart? Do you want to get a taxi there?'

'No, I'll be fine walking, if we take it slowly. It's not far, is it?'

'Are you sure? Don't overdo it.' He puts an arm round me, kisses my cheek, and fetches my long red coat from the hall.

'It's a good thing I've got a baggy coat isn't it?'

We set off arm in arm on the slow walk to King's College Hospital, grey sky overhead, uneven paving stones under our feet.

We arrive at the Ultrasound Department on the sixth floor, where there is a small reception desk and a corridor with plastic chairs. Everything seems to be grey, even the walls. A few other pregnant women are waiting. The nurse says I look very pale and finds me a seat while she tries to find details of my appointment. She says her name is Liz; she seems very sympathetic. I must look terrible. Dr Wilson* is there to meet me. He is about my age, with fair hair and glasses. Kind but conventional, I decide. Liz ushers me into a room with a high couch and what looks like a black-and-white TV screen. I have to lie on my back, pull down my huge maternity trousers and pull up my top. The ultrasound probe presses uncomfortably into my tight, swollen abdomen, which Liz has liberally squirted with a jelly-like substance. She is now staring intently at the TV screen. Dr Wilson doesn't seem to approve of my home birth. He asks me how old I am.

'Thirty-seven.'

'You know at your age, with your first baby and severe polyhydramnios, you should be in hospital,' he says, as if I have personally insulted him.

Where does he think I am? I wonder. I remember I don't like hospitals.

'How many weeks did you say you were?' he asks, looking at my enormous abdomen.

'30 weeks tomorrow.'

'Is that from a scan?'

'No, I didn't have a scan.'

'You didn't have a scan? Why not?'

'It wasn't necessary. The baby's heartbeat was developing fine. I'd had a Bart's Test and scored 1 in 900.'

God, I could do without having to explain that I'm not a sheep.

---

*Not his real name

'Well, if you didn't have a scan, how do you know you're not a month out?'

'Because I know when I conceived.'

'When was your last period?'

'The second of May; but I'm counting it as the ninth because I ovulated on the 23rd – three weeks later.'

I am getting a bit fed up with this conversation. I know he is only concerned about me, and lives in the kind of world where there are certain medical things you do – better to be safe than sorry – but it's wearing. I am frightened and vulnerable enough. Thank goodness Nick is here beside me. It seems to be dawning on Doctor Wilson that I'm not stupid, however, and he adds, 'You'd be surprised how many women do get it wrong, you know, which is why a dating scan is so helpful.'

And how many dating scans are wrong? As he peers at the screen over Liz's shoulder I try not to put him in my mental box of Doctors-who-don't-listen-to-women. He is peering at the screen like a little boy being shown a new computer game.

'That's interesting; it looks like another sac.'

The shadowy grey shape looks totally indistinguishable to me.

'What is it?' I ask, feeling a kind of apprehensive curiosity about this strange unknown world inside my body.

'Well, it looks as if you may have conceived twins and one died in the embryo stage, leaving the empty sac. But I'm not very good at reading these things,' he adds. 'We'll have to ask someone else.'

I am still wondering what an empty sac has got to do with swelling up like a water balloon, when they call in Jill, who is obviously more experienced.

'Oh, no, it always has that bit on the screen, this machine. It's something to do with the angle. But she's definitely got polyhydramnios; we'd better send her up to Kypros.'

As she helps me off the scanning table, she says, 'Kypros can sound a bit abrupt sometimes, but don't be put off. It's just his manner; he doesn't mean it.'

I seem to be getting more care and understanding than the other women there; I begin to let in uneasily the realisation that there really is something wrong with my pregnancy. I am just taking everything as it comes and not letting myself imagine what is going to happen next. I feel like a child going to the dentist for the first time, not knowing quite what to expect but suspecting it isn't going to be pleasant.

On the way up in the lift, Nick asks Dr Wilson who Kypros is.

'Kypros Nicolaides. He's the director of the Harris Birthright Centre, on the ninth floor. It's a specialist unit, so women are referred from all over the country. Kypros really manages to do his own thing up there; it's like his own little kingdom really. You know, it's amazing, he was in the same year as me at medical school, and now look at him; he's on television, he's invited to speak at international conferences. He was a surgeon for a while, but he wasn't too brilliant at it, so he was transferred to ultrasound and he turned out to be this total genius.' His voice is full of awe. 'He's totally eccentric, too. He's Greek, of course.'

The ninth floor is quite different. Even though we still have to sit in the long corridor, the chairs are comfortable, and there is carpet on the floor, tall plants, a tank of goldfish, and a section with toys for children to play with.

'This is nicer, isn't it?' Nick remarks. 'And look, no one's wearing uniform.'

This is not like my idea of a hospital; I feel more relaxed here. I lie down along a row of chairs and put my head in Nick's lap. I am too uncomfortable sitting down. I wonder why I have more confidence in a place like this rather than the sixth floor. I suppose it's because someone has thought about what would make the surroundings nice for the patients, so I assume that we are going to be respected more as people who are responsible for their own bodies and not as just a set of symptoms.

This hospital, like all others, is slightly too warm for comfort, and there is a constant humming noise like the engine on a ship.

It reminds me of crossing the Indian Ocean with my mother, at the age of six, on our way to Malaya, when the air-conditioning broke down. Our cabin had no portholes.

'Was it hotter than this?' asks Nick, as I remove another layer.

'Almost.'

'See – there are no portholes here, either.'

There are a number of other couples waiting, and each time someone walks down the corridor, either arriving or leaving, or a name is called out, all eyes turn to follow what is happening. We are like spectators at Wimbledon. I notice that nobody is reading, and a lot of the couples are holding hands. There seem to be few women on their own. I find myself remembering how a friend described being in the waiting room of a cancer unit: the tension and sense of resignation. The atmosphere here doesn't seem like that, so I'm not particularly bothered that this memory has come back so vividly; but I notice it keeps coming back.

It is about an hour later that a tall woman doctor with a Spanish accent calls me from the top of the corridor. She leads us into a room at the end, followed by the silent eyes of the remaining Wimbledon crowd, and starts scanning me. She seems nice, but doesn't tell me her name or really say anything to either of us. It is beginning to get quite uncomfortable lying on my back, and with my over-stretched abdomen, the scanning probe feels painful. I try to ask her questions, but she isn't very forthcoming; she just concentrates on the screen. I feel the strain of all the anxiety pressing more heavily on me. I hold Nick's hand tightly and ask him for some Rescue Remedy. It is comforting to have something familiar, the little brandy-flavoured drops on my tongue, and I am so glad to have Nick with me. He doesn't say much; nor do I. He alternately watches the screen and looks at me to see if I am all right, and continues to hold my hand. We are both just waiting.

Then a man comes in and starts scanning me. He doesn't introduce himself either, but talks to the woman doctor in a low tone, so that we can't hear what they are saying. It unnerves me a bit. I feel as if my body is being treated as not mine, as nothing to do with me. The male doctor has a foreign accent, so I wonder if he might be Kypros, but he doesn't fit my picture. He hasn't enough presence somehow. I try to think of things to say to Nick to break the increasingly funereal atmosphere. It seems to last a long time. It is dark in the room; the green, patterned curtains are drawn to keep out the dull December light and the focal point becomes the strange grey shapes moving on the little screen as the probe is moved around on my aching abdomen.

At last the man (later I learn his name is Anthony) turns to me and explains in a quiet, careful way that the reason there is too much fluid is because the baby isn't swallowing properly. If there is too much or too little amniotic fluid, it is a warning sign. What's coming next? I wonder. I already know what he's just told me.

'This could either mean,' he continues, 'that there's a problem with the oesophagus or that there is some other reason why the baby is not swallowing, but it is difficult to see with all this fluid. So I would like to drain some of it off, by putting a needle in your abdomen.'

This is what I have been dreading. I realise I have suspected that this was the only way to relieve the pressure and the pain, but I have pushed it to the back of my mind. Now it is in front of me, I start shaking all over. There seems to be nothing I can do about it. The tears start too. 'Can you just give me time?' I ask. I am clutching Nick's hand tightly.

'Certainly. I can't make you do it, of course, but if you don't have it done, you will go into labour soon anyway. And you will feel much better after you've lost some fluid. Look at how much it's hurting now.'

I know what he is saying makes sense, but I am numbed with shock, the stress of not knowing what is wrong, and the dread of this needle. To think that I shuddered at the thought of a mere amniocentesis!

I ask if I can call Nicky, and the Spanish doctor shows us into a little room with a desk and telephone. All I can do is cry, so Nick phones Nicky's beeper number and leaves a message. I slowly cry and shake my way through a box of Kleenex, while Nick holds my hand. I feel like a little child. 'I want Nicky! I don't want a needle in me!' my mind is crying in terror. And as the numbness gradually wears off, I know I will have to go through with the draining, not just to relieve my own pain, but to save our baby. I have to trust them, because I know I can't contemplate living with the thought that I could have saved my baby's life and didn't. Nicky soon calls back and Nick explains to her what is happening.

'She's coming straight away, but she's only got the bike, so she'll be about three-quarters of an hour,' he tells me.

Soon a young woman with curly fair hair and a kind smile comes to ask how I am, and listens understandingly.

'I'm Ruth,' she says. 'I'm the senior midwife here. Just stay here as long as you want,' she adds.

When I feel a bit better, I go over to the loo, which is round the corner, past the scan rooms. As I come out, I pass a man with black hair and a black beard talking to two or three other men. They are obviously listening to him as someone with authority. I know it is Kypros. He glances at me and gives a quick nod as if he feels he ought to know me.

I go back to the little office and wait with Nick. After a while Ruth comes and tells me that Douglas Salvesen, the senior registrar, wants to scan me. We go through into another, larger room, where a young fair-haired doctor is sitting at a bigger, newer-looking and obviously superior scanning machine. Two women are standing discreetly at the foot of the scanning table.

'Hello,' he says as we come in, and introduces the women. 'They are visiting doctors. I hope you don't mind them observing.'

'No, I like an audience,' I say as I climb on the scanning table. Having had a cry, I make jokes to try to stop the shaking. It puts me a little bit more in charge of a situation that I am beginning to feel is out of my hands. And it gives me courage, helping me to experience what is actually happening, rather than slipping into my thoughts, where undesirable fears might be lurking. All my doubts about ultrasound scans have gone out of the window. I'm on a different tramline now. I prepare my abdomen for the third lot of jelly.

After Douglas has examined the screen for a while he explains what he sees. 'It looks as if the baby's got a problem with one lung, the right one. You see here?' We can just about make out the shape of the baby's ribcage and the lung, as he points them out. There is a baby in this strange, grey, silent world. 'Well, I don't know if you can see it with all this fluid,' (he is right, we can't), 'but the diaphragm here is curving up into the area where just the lung should be, so the lung's too small. It looks as if it could be a diaphragmatic hernia, where the diaphragm, instead of being tight, is too long and slack, so that the organs from below push up into the pleural cavity and stop the lung developing.'

'Why isn't the baby swallowing enough?' I ask, noticing how calm I sound.

'Well, I can't see clearly, but I think it's just that the oesophagus is getting a bit constricted by the pressure on the lung.'

'What can be done?' I ask.

'The baby will have to have an operation, a few days after birth, to shorten the diaphragm. They will have to keep the baby in an incubator at birth, and won't operate till it's stable.'

'What's the success rate?'

'Statistically, about 50-50, but it is impossible to tell till birth, because some babies are in a worse condition than others. The operation works; the factor is whether they are in a condition to have the operation.'

Now I can feel the tears welling up uncontrollably. I cover my face with my arm and for a moment sob into it. 'I've waited so long for this baby.' There is a kind of sympathetic hush in the room. They know I have. I appreciate so much that Douglas and Ruth are honest and give me room just to go through whatever I am going through, without trying to cheer me up or make bland comments. Nick is still holding my hand. I suspect that he's pretty upset, but he doesn't show it. He is just looking at me anxiously.

The sobs last about a minute, while everyone in the room stands quietly. Then I turn to Douglas.

'What happens next?' I ask. I need all the knowledge I can get, in this frightening, unknown new world.

'We'll give you a cordocentesis, so that we can test for chromosomal abnormalities. It is just a very fine needle inserted in your abdomen.'

'How long does that take?'

'About two minutes,' says Douglas. 'And then we'll put a slightly larger needle in to drain off some of this fluid.'

'Will it hurt?'

'No – it's like a needle in your arm,' he says lightly. I don't believe him.

'Can I wait till Nicky arrives?' I ask. I am shaking and brushing the tears from my eyes; it is so confronting actually talking about it all.

'Yes, OK.'

Ruth and Nick help me off the scan table to a chair at the side of the room. I am crying and shaking. Now the worst fears have been spoken, and I have to confront them both at once. Later our baby may die and now I am going to have needles stuck in me.

Ruth brings us each a mug of tea. It isn't the plastic powdered stuff from the machine; it is real tea. I sip it and sob. She squats on the floor beside me, holding my hand.

'Don't worry. You don't have to do anything till Nicky's here. But I'm afraid we have to ask you to go next door, as there are other patients waiting to come in here.' She says all this very gently and reassuringly, with no sense of rushing me.

Then she and Nick help me through to the room next door, which contains two monitoring machines of some kind, a bed with a white sheet on it and an armchair. I sit on the bed and

Nick sits next to me. He puts his arm around me and we sip our tea quietly, with me stopping to cry every so often. The reality of what is happening is sifting through slowly, bit by bit. It is like regaining a limb that has been frozen with anaesthetic – except that the limb is my mind.

We wait there a long time, watching people go in and out of the scanning room, looking at the dials on the monitors, and gazing at the green curtains with their big Sixties pattern, about six inches too short, as if they'd shrunk when they were washed. We talk to comfort each other, we drink sweet hot chocolate out of the machine, and we watch the daylight gradually fade and the lights come on over London.

Eventually Nicky arrives, sympathetic and consoling, and asks us if we've had lunch. No, we haven't, we realise. The canteen is closed, but she manages to find us a packet of cheese sandwich biscuits. We devour them with relish, happy to concentrate on something as ordinary as the salty, cheesy taste of the biscuits.

At about five o'clock, Douglas comes in and says they can't wait any longer. I have to come in now. It is the first time he has asked, so I sense it is a bit confronting for him too, and he is trying to sound firm as much for himself as for me. It works, though. We follow him next door.

Douglas hands me two forms to sign, giving my consent for the cordocentesis and the draining. Next to the line at the bottom, it says 'Signature of the mother'. I burst into tears again. I really am a mother, not just a pregnant woman. This is my child. It is the first formal recognition of my motherhood, but not one I ever wanted or expected.

I climb back on the scanning table and stare up at the polystyrene ceiling tiles, while more jelly is squirted on my exposed, rounded abdomen. I ask Nicky to stand on one side of my head and hold my right hand, and Nick to stand on the other side and hold my left hand.

'Gosh, I'm nervous!' I say.

'Just keep breathing,' says Nicky. 'Deep breaths into your tummy.' I take some deep breaths and can feel my abdomen making the scan probe move up and down as Douglas looks for the cord and the right place to put in the needle. I feel the cold wipe of anaesthetic on a patch near my navel.

'Now just breathe a bit more lightly,' says Douglas, 'to keep still where I'm putting the needle in.'

'Keep talking,' I say, to block out the thoughts.

'What about?' asks Nicky as I start breathing more into my chest.

'Your course. How's your course going? What are you doing at the moment?'

I concentrate all my mind on trying to take in her answer and keep completely still as I feel a fine sliver of steel pushed gently through layers of muscle. I presume she tells me about the lectures and seminars she has had, and I know I answer and ask more questions, but all I am aware of is my whole body being alert, suspended and waiting for the moment when Douglas says, 'That's it. I've done it.'

The relief! I feel slightly giggly. One horrible bit is over, and it hasn't been too bad. But I sense that the draining will be much worse than the cordocentesis.

'Now, we'll take you next door again for the next part.'

We all troop back into the other room and I am asked to lie on my back on the bed. One of the monitors is turned on. It is a little scan machine with a small screen. Douglas starts scanning me again, and pressing my abdomen gently, sort of testing the ground, I think. I watch Nick. He is watching Douglas apprehensively. It must be worse for him, in a way, watching me go through all this. No wonder he's so quiet.

'Nick, come and hold my hand,' I say. He stands beside me while I look up at the ceiling. It has the same polystyrene tiles as the other room, with grey squiggles on. They remind me of my bottom when I put on lots of weight at the age of 19.

'Do you know you've got stretch marks on your ceiling, Douglas?'
He looks up and gives a little chuckle.

'Oh, yes.'

Nicky is standing at the end of the bed, in front of the hand basin
and mirror. We just keep talking for the sake of talking, while I wait
for the moment. I feel the swab of anaesthetic, then –

'Aaagh!' I cry out, as I feel the pain of something being stabbed
into my abdomen. And the pain goes on. 'This is horrible,' I say,
keeping my eyes fixed on Nicky and then going straight on with
the conversation about cheese biscuits or Advanced Midwifery
Courses or whatever it is. I notice in a second that saying it is
horrible brings it too much to the front of my mind, and I can feel
a wave of panic threatening to surface. Staying in our conversation
keeps it at bay. I feel Douglas sticking something soft on to me
with tape, and glance down to see a square of tape and pads of
cotton wool. There is a long rod coming out of it – it looks like
one of my grandmother's knitting needles – with a plastic tube at
the top leading over the side of the bed into something I can't see.
I quickly put my head back on the pillows again. I am breathing in
my chest. Even the small movement of breathing makes the needle
move slightly so I can feel it.

'How long will this take?' I ask.

'About an hour,' says Douglas. There is nothing for it but to lie here
talking, keeping calm and not panicking. The pain doesn't ease up.
It just keeps hurting. I keep talking, trying to joke, concentrating
on being with words, and Nick's hand in mine, not with the pain
in my body nor the thoughts in my head.

I am lying on the bed with this large rod sticking out of my
abdomen when Kypros comes in, followed by Douglas and Ruth.
He is obviously in command. He looks at me and stops.

'I know you, don't I? Where did we meet?'

'Well, I saw you just now in the corridor.'

'No, I'm sure we met before that. Did you park in the front car
park?'

'No.'

'Well, never mind.'

He sits down on the edge of the bed and presses my abdomen briefly.

'Are you Cypriot Greek or Greek Greek?' I ask as he runs the scanner over me. I don't want to think about the pain I feel when the bed moves even the slightest.

'Cypriot,' he replies. 'Why?'

'I was born in Cyprus.'

'What were you doing there?' he asks, managing to look at the scanner screen as well as listen.

'My father was doing research on locusts.'

Douglas and the others seem to find this funny for some reason and laugh.

'Could you possibly sit on the chair, please?' I ask. He looks at me, not understanding what I am asking. 'I can feel every movement down this tube,' I explain. He gives a quick smile to himself and moves on to the chair. Then he looks straight at me and says, 'Now, you need to be prepared for the fact that this baby probably won't live.'

'Yes,' I say. Perhaps this is what Jill meant about him being abrupt, but I appreciate his being straight. I feel nothing can get worse than it is now. I am prepared for anything.

'It looks as if the baby has a diaphragmatic hernia, which means that the lung doesn't have room to form properly. And it's on the right side, which makes it more problematic, as that's the bigger lung. I can't really give you an accurate prognosis till we've drained off some of this fluid, but I would say at this stage that you may have a 30% chance of the baby surviving, with an operation after birth. I'll scan you when this is finished.'

He is off, and the waves threaten to close in again.

'OK, what shall we talk about now? Can you tell Nicky about the book you are illustrating, Nick?'

After about half an hour, Nicky receives a message from Katrina saying that one of their other patients is in labour and it is reaching the stage where she really needs her there.

'Will you be all right without me?' Nicky asks.

Clear that we are OK, she tells Ruth that she is going, and leaves. Nick is very quiet, though I can see he is making an effort to talk, because it helps me. He tells me later that it was shocking, watching me being drained. But his presence makes all the difference. I can see he is watching everything that is happening to me, and if I don't ask questions about the interventions, he always does.

After another half an hour, it starts to hurt much more than before. I tell Nick, and ask him to get Ruth. I can feel myself sweating slightly as I concentrate on the breath going in and out of my chest and hold the tension of not panicking. Douglas comes in, followed by Ruth. He picks up the bag that is on the end of the tube, on the floor, and looks at it.

'Yes, that'll do.' He kneels down and pulls the needle out. It hurts like hell, but this time the pain is mixed with relief.

'How much was that?' I ask, breathing fast.

'About two litres,' he tells me.

He pulls the cotton wool and tape off my abdomen and throws it in the bin. Then he holds a bit of antiseptic cotton wool over the hole and asks me to hold it for a while. I can feel the relief and sense of exhaustion now it is over. I wonder whether the needle started to hurt more as the tension in my abdomen receded. Maybe the tightness caused by the polyhydramnios acted like a slight anaesthetic.

'Come back into the scan room as soon as you can,' says Douglas, and leaves.

I try to move, and feel the pain shoot over my abdomen as soon as I tense my muscles to sit up.

'Ow!' I cry. Ruth comes round to help me.

'Try turning on your side first. You poor thing, you must really be sore.'

They help me up slowly. I feel as if I have been beaten all over.

Every muscle in my torso aches, and all of them seem to be connected to the ones bruised by the draining needle. Nick and Ruth virtually carry me under the arms into the scan room. I feel like a war victim.

'Well, I certainly feel lighter,' I remark as I am hauled on to the scanning table again. Humour is my only resource. I am going to use it wherever I can. As soon as everything is set up, Kypros strides in and takes Douglas's place at the screen. I can tell immediately from the way he handles the probe and reads the screen that he is in a class of his own. If anyone can see clearly what is wrong, he can. After looking for a few minutes, with everyone in the room watching the screen, he says, 'Well, this looks a little better now we've cleared some of the fluid. You're right, Douglas. It looks like a diaphragmatic hernia, with slight pleural oedema on the right side.'

'What's pleural oedema?' I ask.

'It's fluid round the lung, inside the chest,' he explains. 'Look, you see here? This is the chest.'

I can see clearly the little ribs and some shapes inside.

'This area here is the lung. And you see this dark patch?' He indicates a thin, dark area round the edge of the lung, inside the ribs. 'That's the oedema.'

That's my little baby on the screen. That's my baby.

He shows us the misshapen diaphragm, which is distinguishable now, then he turns to us.

'You see? I should say your baby's chance of survival is about 50-50. Now, Ruth will arrange for you to have an appointment with the Paediatric Surgeon so you can ask any questions, and Chrissy, you should come in next week to be drained again.'

I have been hoping that it would only need to be done once, but at the back of my mind I knew once wouldn't be enough. After all, the baby still isn't swallowing. But I don't need to think about it now. I just want to go home, to be with Nick and Cleo and my safe bed.

'Now your job,' says Kypros, 'is to keep this baby in for as long as you can, to give the lungs the maximum chance to develop. Ideally till 37 or 38 weeks. So each time you get drained there is a small percentage risk that you'll go into labour, because the muscle goes into spasm, but if you get too big again you risk the body thinking it's time to give birth, and going into labour that way. So, you know what your job is. Off you go, and we'll see you in a week.'

Ruth hands me two letters, printed out from the computer.

'I'll call you when we receive the results of the cordocentesis,' she says. 'They're usually back in a week. Take care of her, won't you, Nick?'

She smiles understandingly and puts an arm round my shoulders.

'I certainly will. And thanks for all your support today.'

'Yes, it made such a difference,' I add.

'That's all right. It's what we're here for,' she replies.

It is nearly seven o'clock. We have been in the hospital for six and a half hours. We walk slowly down the empty corridor and out through the double doors.

Chapter Four

The Project

Responsibility starts with saying you are cause in the matter.

Responsibility is not burden, fault, praise, blame, credit, shame or guilt. In responsibility, there is no evaluation of good or bad, right or wrong. There is simply what's so, and your stand.

Being responsible starts with the willingness to deal with a situation from the point of view that you are the generator of what you do, what you have and what you are. That is not the truth. It is a place to stand.

No one can make you responsible, nor can you impose responsibility on another.

It is a grace you give yourself – an empowering context that leaves you with a say in the matter of life.

I walk into our bedroom, and Cleo looks up anxiously from the bed. Everything looks the same as it did when we left in the morning, but in that short time we have been through so much. I sit down and look at Nick.

'I don't want our baby to die,' I say.

'Nor do I,' Nick says, and he hugs me as I cry in his arms. It has finally sunk in: our baby might die.

Strangely, I don't find myself thinking 'Why me?' or 'What did I do wrong?' as I did with my miscarriages, till enough people told me that every woman who has a miscarriage has those thoughts and there is no point in taking any notice of them. I suppose this situation is so serious I am not letting in thoughts like that. Maybe I know, as perhaps we all do, that thoughts like that are so disempowering. I knew not to take seriously certain thoughts that seem to enter our head unbidden, but I hadn't fully realised that our minds, in times of crisis, can actually keep them out altogether.

'How are you, darling?' I ask Nick. 'You've been looking after me all the time; are you OK?'

'Yes, I'm fine. I just want to take care of you and the baby.'

We sit hugging for a while, then I say, 'What are we going to do?'

It is almost rhetorical, but Nick answers, 'Well, let's make it into a kind of project, to do everything we can to save her. Like we did with the portraits. So, you know, we have Kypros and the others on the team, and Fred and Jeremy.' Fred's our homeopath.

Yes, a project would give me an anchor, something to focus on through this uncertain future.

'I could ask Phillida about that healer who cured her of M.E., the one in the New Forest,' I say. 'That's what to do: just do everything, and it will either work or it won't, but at least we'll know that we left nothing out and have nothing to regret.'

I phone my mother. She knows I have been in pain for a while, but is naturally shocked and saddened to hear about the problems with the baby, and what I have been through that day.

'Oh, my dear, I'm so sorry,' she says.

'Could you pass it on to the rest of the family?' I ask.

'Of course I will. I'll phone Sue now. Take care, won't you, dear?'

We go to bed early. Before I fall asleep, I think how it must be for my mother, knowing her daughter is suffering, unable to do anything about it. There have never been any problems with pregnancy on either side of the family till now. She must be very anxious. At least she knows I am being well taken care of by Nick, and that I am with a knowledgeable consultant. Strange, I am the same age now as she was when she had me, 37 years ago in Cyprus Mines Hospital, Pendayia, during a hot Mediterranean summer.

Here I am, in a dark, damp, English winter, experiencing procedures and equipment unheard of in her day.

I appreciate our bed so much tonight. No medical instruments or needles in the room, our familiar things around us, and Cleo curled up on the duvet. It feels peaceful and safe. And I know I need every bit of peace and safety I can get, to strengthen me in the face of what we have taken on. I realise that, for as long as it takes, I will constantly have to imagine myself into the future and look back, looking for what I might regret later if I don't do it now. And it would be far easier not to think like that, just to live from day to day, blocking out worrying thoughts, and hoping that things will turn out. But I recognise the cost might be to spend the rest of my life thinking 'If only…' – a cost I am not prepared to pay.

I start the project the next day, sitting in bed. I phone my homeopath, the healer in the New Forest and my nutritionist doctor, who I had found through an organisation called Foresight – an ironic name, it seems now – after my two miscarriages. They are both understanding, and the healer asks me to write a letter, because he needs something of mine to focus the energy on. Nick is leading a seminar that night for Landmark Education, an extraordinary organisation that runs transformational courses. When he gets home he tells me how he has talked with the participants about the baby, and our project to have him or her live. He is looking bright-eyed and vulnerable.

'People shared how shocked they were, and how inspired by us. Lots of them said if we needed any help, even with shopping or cooking, just ask them. One woman is meditating for us, and someone else is asking a whole convent of nuns to pray for us!'

Two days after the call with my mother, a card and a parcel arrives from my sister:

'Dear Sissy,

We're all really sorry that you and the teeny one are having problems. It must be really awful for you. If positive thoughts winging their way through the airwaves have anything to do with it (s)he will be fine. Take heart and take care Sissy, we all send you lots and lots of love and a tacky old pinny (well not very) which you might possibly find useful.

Sue x x x'

I sniff back the tears as I open the parcel to find a blue needlecord pinafore dress. I wear it a lot from now on.

⌒

News spreads fast and supportive phone calls and cards start to pour in. Our friends are shocked, saddened and very understanding. One friend tells Nick that when she heard there was something wrong with the baby she had been very upset, and had then thought, 'Well, if I were God and I had a baby who needed a lot of love and care and really wonderful parents, I'd send it to Nick and Chrissy.'

December 9th 1991. Nicky takes me to King's to be officially booked in to have my baby in hospital. As we are leaving the antenatal clinic I see Dr Wilson coming in at the door. He hasn't seen me, so I say 'Hello' to him. He looks at me blankly for a moment, and then remembers who I am.

'Oh, yes, of course; hello. Come to book in, have you? So it wasn't twins was it, but a diaphragmatic hernia. Well, you're still an interesting case.'

I don't know whether to be amused or annoyed. I suppose he just put his thoughts on external speaker. Nicky and I exchange a look and a smile as we walk to the lift. It doesn't matter what he's like.

Our next visit is to the Fred Still Ward, the intensive care unit for babies. Angela, the other midwife from the Harris Birthright Centre, who we haven't met before, greets us. She is young and beautiful, with silky, dark shoulder-length hair, a rather French elegance in her clothes, and a warm, compassionate smile. She shows us how to wash our hands in the special sterilising fluid before we go in, and introduces us to the various doctors we meet.

There are two rooms, each containing several incubators, and a multitude of machines, wires and other equipment. I can hear a constant low hum, and electronic clicks. The rooms are very warm and the lights are low. It could have been any time of day or night.

'Here you are, darling,' says Angela, 'this is where your baby will come when it's born.' Her voice is reassuring and intimate, without being intrusive.

We look into the first incubator. A baby, only a few days old, wearing just a nappy, is lying on his back, asleep, with a couple of wires taped on to his little wrists. Angela explains that he has just had an operation and is doing fine. The baby in the next one is very small.

'Premature?' I ask quietly.

'No, just underweight,' Angela replies. 'She didn't grow properly inside her mother for some reason. It happens sometimes.'

I look at this miniature, perfectly formed, wrinkled little baby, slowly moving her arms and legs, and opening her mouth to make a slight, whimpering cry. She seems so alone and helpless, and, despite all the warmth of the incubator, I feel she needs to be held and cuddled. I talk to her softly, but she doesn't seem to hear me. A woman in a dressing gown is sitting by another incubator, holding her baby in her arms, with two wires attached to its little wrists. We see more babies, mostly premature, but it is the last one that stays in my memory. This baby is really tiny, and is just lying, breathing heavily, with a tube going into her mouth.

'Oxygen,' says Angela softly. 'She was born long before her lungs had finished developing. Poor little thing, she shouldn't be outside.'

When I get home, I lie on the bed, and Nick goes to the kitchen to make me some tea. I am aware that I have a baby about the same size as the premature ones I had just seen, safe inside me. Safe till the birth. Safe till she tries to breathe. I know how crucial those first few days of life are and, of course, the first few hours and minutes, the time for bonding, when I won't be able to put the baby on my front to cuddle. But what matters is just being there, being a mother all the time. The birth; what a long way from the one I hoped for. In fact, the whole picture is so far from what I wanted or imagined, but as there is nothing that can be done about it, I imagine how I can do the best for my baby. I try to get myself used to the fact that I will probably have to spend days living in the hospital, sleeping in the maternity ward, and visiting the Fred Still ward as often as I possibly can. I decide I will stay with my baby all my waking hours till he or she is better.

Nick comes back with a mug of tea and a slice of ginger cake, so I sit up and tell him about the visit to the hospital. He smiles and shakes his head when I tell him about Dr Wilson. He looks at me quietly and seriously while I tell him about the Fred Still ward.

'What are you thinking?' I ask.

'I don't know, really. Just picturing it,' he replies. He is absorbing it all, and I feel a rush of gratitude for his love and understanding, his eternal support.

'Thank you for the cake,' I say, with tears in my eyes.

I lie dozing on the bed, picturing myself in the middle of the night in that warm room, wearing a dressing gown, and holding my baby next to her incubator, alone with the soft whirs and clicks of all the machinery. I always picture a baby girl, for some reason. I know I won't be able to breast-feed her, as she will need to be oxygenated, but I can pump my own milk, which will be fed to her. I can't think past that point. I can't imagine taking her home, buying her clothes, feeding her, her growing to be a toddler. All I can think of are those endless timeless days and nights, before and after our baby's operation.

December 11th 1991. I know I will have to be drained again. My tummy is large and hard, though not quite as bad as before. I am dreading it.

'Well, what can we do to lighten it up a bit?' Nick asks.

'We could find out the baby's sex.'

'OK.'

We look at each other.

'I hope it's a girl,' says Nick.

'So do I.' It's like confessing a secret.

On the way up in the lift we bump into, predictably, I think, Dr Wilson. I wonder what he's going to say this time. He smiles cheerfully and asks, 'How are you, then?'

'Nervous,' I say. I'm sure my face looks tense.

'Oh, there's nothing to worry about. Your baby stands a good chance; the surgeons are excellent.'

'That's not what I'm nervous about,' I say. 'It's the draining.' Then I add, 'It's very painful,' in case it hasn't occurred to him.

'It won't hurt this time,' he says dismissively. 'You were pretty upset last time, remember.'

I don't say anything. It is one of those occasions when you think of a dozen dry, witty answers afterwards, but I see in that moment that he, personally, hasn't made up that reply. It is just What a Doctor Says. His assertion is patently not based on experience, but, I muse, perhaps some women believe what male doctors tell them about the kinds of pain that men can't have experienced. Perhaps those doctors are saying what they think women want to hear. But telling someone they are not going to feel pain when it is clear they are going to doesn't diminish it; if anything it increases it, because they then have, in addition, the feeling of not being heard or understood. They are also, particularly if they are English, liable to stop themselves crying out, thereby intensifying the agony. My fear is making my thoughts venomous. I say nothing as Nick chats to Dr Wilson.

'I was just coming up to Harris Birthright, so I'll come along with you,' Dr Wilson says.

Damn.

It is clearly very busy that morning; the corridor is full, and Ruth and Angela are trying to be helpful to everybody. When Kypros summons either of them, they almost run up the corridor. Angela passes and stops briefly to say affectionately, 'Hello, darlings. How are you?'

We don't have to wait long, though. I'm used to the whole jelly procedure by now. Dr Wilson asks Douglas if he can watch, and looks interested as Douglas shows him the diaphragm and lungs.

'I see the baby's still breech,' he remarks.

'Yes,' said Douglas. 'It might still turn around; there's still an excess of amniotic fluid.'

Dr Wilson is obviously impressed with the sophistication of the machines, but also fascinated by any chance of Solving the Mystery of the Interesting Case. Nicky has told me, 'Midwives see all kinds of pregnancies, but mainly normal ones. Doctors see anything that isn't going normally. That's what they learn about.' I don't know if it's still true, but I heard that in China, you pay your doctor when you are well. When you get ill you stop, because he's failing in his job. But in the West, medicine seems to deal in ill-health not in health.

While Douglas is scanning me, Ruth comes up and says, 'We've got the results of the cordocentesis, and there's no chromosomal abnormality.'

'Oh, thank you,' I reply. 'That's good to know.' My spirits rise a little and I manage to smile at Nick.

After Douglas has looked for a while and given various measurements to Ruth at the computer, I choose a strategic moment and ask him, 'Can you tell us what sex the baby is?' He keeps his eyes on the screen.

'Oh, I can't do that,' he says, moving the probe round on my abdomen. I am not sure if he is joking. There is a pause, so I continue, 'If it's a boy, we were thinking of calling him Douglas.'

'Oh, I wouldn't call your baby Douglas if I were you,' he replies.

'Why not?' I ask. 'It's a nice name.'

'Because it's a little girl,' he replies, and grins.

'Really?' Nick and I both exclaim, relieved and delighted. 'Can we see?'

'Look!'

The scanner seems to tilt her over backwards so we can see between her little curled up legs.

'She's a little Ruthie!' says Douglas.

'So she is!' said Ruth.

A little girl! I am so pleased. It makes her that much more real. I can authentically visualise her now, and it clarifies the bond between us, somehow. I feel the probe move around again. 'Look,' says Nick softly, and squeezes my hand. I look up to see her move her tiny thumb towards her mouth. Her face isn't that clear: she looks like a little astronaut, moving slowly and silently on the television screen. I feel a thrill of excitement. It is strange that we can see her, but she has no idea that we can. She is in another world. How odd that I am so much more familiar with the world outside my body than the world inside. I can't imagine what it must be like to be her, and yet I feel so close and connected.

I try to remember her face as we are led into the room where I was drained the last time, Dr Wilson still following us around. I lie down and look at the familiar mirror above the wash basin, the straight black angle-poise light without a bulb in, fixed to the wall, and the polystyrene tiles on the ceiling with their grey squiggles. Nick and Dr Wilson stand at the foot of the bed, chatting away while Anthony scans me and prepares my abdomen. I am disappointed that the unsmiling Anthony is going to do this and not Douglas. I am also horribly aware that only I am going through this ordeal.

'This is good,' Anthony tells me. 'The fluid hasn't built up as much as we expected.' Well that is something to be pleased about, but I can't let it in. I put it aside to think about later. A woman arrives and introduces herself as Liz, a visiting midwife, who is going to observe, if that is all right. I say it is fine. I notice she looks the type who will be very comforting; she is warm and gentle.

'Quick, let's talk about what we planned,' I say to Nick. 'What are we going to call her?'

'OK,' he says. 'Angela, Alice, Alexis...'

I let out a cry as Anthony pushes the needle into my abdomen. It is even worse than I remember. I try to concentrate on the name game as Anthony wraps the gauze around the needle and tapes the pad onto my abdomen.

'Now B,' I say. 'I can't think of any B's. I don't like B anyway...' The pain is overwhelming. Even though I am lying down, I can feel my head emptying as if I am fainting. It is a terrible feeling.

'I can't take this,' I say. 'It's too much.' I can feel my heart beating with fear. But Liz has already moved forward and holds me as she moves one of the pillows so I am lying flatter.

'Hold my hand,' I manage to say, and grip hers tight. An anchor.

'Now just take slow breaths, like this,' she says, and as I copy her there is a slight relief in having something to distract my mind. Nick gets me a glass of water and puts Rescue Remedy in it, so I can sip it. Just keeping going, taking one breath after another, seems to take all my mental strength. An hour drags by, as I try to keep my mind off the tremendous pain and the panic threatening to well up. Dr Wilson left soon after I said, 'I can't take this', so Nick and Liz and I keep the conversation going somehow. Nick tells her what happened last time we were here, we tell her where we live, about Cleo, and anything else we can think of. Every now and then Anthony or Ruth pop in to see how the draining is going, and I ask how much longer? Suddenly it becomes even worse. I know it has to end. I can't take any more.

'Nick, can you fetch Ruth or Angela for me?' I say.

He goes straight out, and a moment later is back, followed by

Douglas.

'1.6 litres,' he says, looking at it. 'That'll do.'

I groan as he pulls the needle out, and removes the tape. 'That was hell,' I say, tears of pain in my eyes. Now it is over, I can cry, without the sobs shaking the needle.

'Poor Chrissy,' he says, washing his hands at the sink, and looking at me. He means it.

We eat the usual cheese biscuits and I sip the Rescue Remedy. Any attempt to sit up is excruciating. I look at Nick, holding my hand and watching me, anxious and still. 'That was horrible.' He nods. He has gone through every minute with me.

After a while Kypros pops his head round the door and says with exaggerated indignation, 'What are you doing in here?'

'Recovering,' I tell him.

'Recovering! Why don't you sit on the chairs in the corridor?' he says, pretending to be annoyed. I don't want to explain why, about the agony of sitting up or moving. I want to stay here.

'Does anyone else need to come in here?' I ask.

'No, no,' he says, and disappears. Ruth and Angela drop in occasionally to see if I am all right: a fair-haired angel and a dark one. It is an hour before I can move without feeling too much pain. I slowly get to my feet, put on my coat, and we go down in the lift. I sit on the wall outside while Nick hails a taxi.

As soon as we get home I phone Nicky.

'I can't go through that again. I can't. What can I do?'

'You must ask for entonox. You shouldn't have to go through pain like that.'

'What's that?' I ask.

'Gas-and-air. You know, women use it in labour. You just breathe it in through a mask.'

'So it can't hurt the baby?'

'No, it disappears out of your system as you breathe it out. It makes you feel a bit drunk, and lessens the pain.'

'Why wasn't I offered it before?' I ask, feeling a bit annoyed.

'I don't know. I think you should have been. Anyway, make sure you get it next time. They can easily borrow it from the labour ward. You won't ever have to go through it without anaesthetic again.'

'Will you come with me?'

'Sure. Just let me know when you're going.'

I go over to the little white wooden box beside the bed, and pull out the drawer at the bottom. It is full of my grandmother's knitting needles. I find one that seems the same size as the draining needle and put it through the correct hole on 'Vicar's Knitting Pin Gauge'. It reads size 24.

But before my next visit I have to go to Guy's Hospital, where they have a specialist unit, for the baby to have a cardiac scan. Her heart is slightly to one side of where it should be, apparently, so I need to have it checked out.

Guy's has a very different feel from King's. It seems to be bare, scruffy, disorganised: not exactly user-friendly. My appointment is in the new tower block, and, after getting off at the right floor, I wander along wide empty linoed corridors, and wait on one of the hard wooden chairs outside a room labelled 'Foetal Cardiac Scans'. There appears to be nobody about and all the doors are shut. It is quite unlike the bustle of the new block at King's. The walls are almost entirely bare, so I read the one poster about cardiac scans in full, then wait. Eventually a woman doctor hurries along the corridor and unlocks the door nearest to me, apologising for keeping me waiting, and explaining that they have to lock every room even if they only leave it for a minute, as there have been so many thefts. The room is small, with the now familiar high white table and scanning machine. After several minutes of careful scrutiny, she says the heart looks all right, but she wants to have Professor Lindsay Allen look at it too. The professor is quiet and meticulous and, I can tell, knows her subject very well. She also says that the heart is fine, 'But,' she adds, 'the baby obviously has other problems, as you realise.'

I ask her why she thinks the heart is not in the right place, and she replies that she can't be sure, but it looks as if it is because of the misshapen diaphragm.

'And the polyhydramnios?' I ask.

'It may just be that her oesophagus is restricted by the heart pushing on it, but, again, I'm only guessing.'

I sit on the train going home thinking how my little baby seems to have become a set of internal organs, which we examine and discuss. I feel a flicker of movement, and remember her slowly moving her thumb to her mouth. While she is inside me nothing has really changed, except in our conversation. To the outside world, I am a pregnant woman, the same as any other, going home on the train, enjoying the sensation of being pregnant. The only difference is that perhaps my enjoyment is more conscious and poignant, suspended as I am in this vivid world of the present, savouring the moments when I'm not in pain.

'We've got to find a name for her,' I tell Nick when I get home.

'She's called Alice,' he replies.

'How do you know?' I ask. He sounds as if she's just told him or something.

'I don't know,' he says. We look at each other.

'She told you, didn't she?' We both laugh.

So, she is called Alice, and from now on we refer to her as Alice to everyone. Of course Nicky and Katrina use her name all the time too, and even Ruth and Angela start to, but the doctors stick to their impersonal 'the baby' or 'your baby'.

I spend much of my time at home lying down, sometimes on the phone to friends and relatives, sometimes reading (though it is hard to concentrate) and sometimes just lying, drifting around in my thoughts and letting any spare energy go to Alice and to keeping my strength up. My bodily state is sometimes merely uncomfortable, sometimes painful.

I feel more and more connected to Alice during this time. It reminds me of those times as a child when I was in the sitting room with my mother; I'd be curled up on the sofa, reading a book, and she'd be in an upright armchair, reading, too, and even though we weren't speaking, there'd be that comfortable sense of presence, of just being together. Or times when my mother would be getting supper and my father and I would be playing cards. We had this wonderful set of Piquet, an old-fashioned card game that my father had played as a child, with strange French words you had to declare. You know there's that feeling, that isn't connected to speaking, or any of the five senses for that matter, but it's very real and it's something we've all experienced. Well, that's what it is like being with Alice, with my little baby swimming slowly in deep waters inside me.

'You know, I was thinking,' I say to Nick. 'Wouldn't it be nice, when this is all over, to draw a portrait of me holding Alice, and we could give it to Kypros to hang in the Harris Birthright Centre.'

I begin to live for skin brushing. It becomes the highlight of my day.

In the last three months, pregnant women's skin often starts to itch. And dry-skin brushing not only helps to clear the body of toxins, but starts to feel really nice. It does for me, anyway. Nick brushes my back upwards with a dry, bristly brush, and then my arms, while I purr like a stroked cat. I manage to persuade him to do it every morning as well as evening, and it becomes something to look forward to. I am almost obsessed.

The nights are the worst, as I wake frequently, often with bad indigestion, which creates a pain down my chest. I feel as if I want to burp but can't. In the end, I buy Gaviscon, a fennel-flavoured indigestion mixture. Though I don't like taking anything that strong, and suspect it isn't helping my body, in the short term it works.

One night, woken as usual by indigestion, I go to the kitchen and make myself some Ovaltine. I appreciate little things like this as real treats. I sit up in bed sipping it, with Nick asleep beside me. It seems so long ago, that bright summer's day when I sat in bed after doing the pregnancy test, with Nick asleep beside me. That was close to the shortest night of the year; now we are even closer to the longest night. We have moved from an outdoor world to an indoor world.

Cleo, unaware I am watching, creeps on to the chair and grabs my black tights in her mouth. Stealthily she drags them across the floor between her legs, meowing with her mouth full. As soon as she notices me, she drops them with a surprised little chirrup and sits looking at me with round, innocent eyes. We hear her doing this every night, and in the morning tights, socks, or my black cardigan are strewn casually on the floor in the bedroom or on the landing: abandoned prey.

The warm blue mug feels comforting as I sit with my hands wrapped around it. I sip the malty chocolate, feeling the steam round my nose. A vivid memory comes into my mind of sitting on a smooth cement wall in the shade of a concrete verandah, holding a glass of sweet milky tea and sipping it slowly, savouring every drop. There weren't many physical comforts in life, in a tribal village in the heart of Gujurat.

We could only have three cups of tea a day at Amari Mandali, because of the expense of heating the water on a bottled gas ring, and because we only had a litre of milk a day between five of us. I loved going to fetch the milk in the morning. I would ride the bicycle along the dry, rutted earth track to the road, and pedal up the hill, weaving between the potholes. The fields were bare, the earth hard and mosaiced by deep cracks. It was April, before the rains, and the few leaves on the trees were dry and crackly. Other people were on the road: tall, upright tribal women, their saris tucked up through their legs to make a trouser-like garment, striding along on their hard, bare feet. There were boys on bicycles, sturdy, solid bicycles with no gears, like mine, sometimes with their sisters sitting side-saddle on the back carrier, and their little brothers on the cross-bar. The girls looked at me with envy and curiosity, riding a bicycle. About a mile up the road I stopped at a little house: a wooden structure with mud-and-dung plaster and factory-made roof-tiles; a house like all the others, but a notice announced that this was the dairy. A queue of children were measuring their little churns of buffalo milk into the big churn and having the amount recorded in a notebook. I had my little empty aluminium churn on the handlebars, and a litre of the milk was measured into it; I was the only person taking milk away. Cycling back was easier, except I had to keep an eye on the gently swinging churn.

Back at the project building, I heated the milk to boiling point on the gas ring to pasteurise it, then let it cool, scooping the skin into a little dish that we kept in the mesh-walled cupboard for making ghee. And to make tea I measured four cups of water, five teaspoons of sugar and some chai masala into a saucepan and heated it with one cup of milk. When it was boiling I stirred in two spoons of finest 'dust tea' and left it to boil for a few minutes. I strained the tea through a metal tea strainer into five glasses and finally settled down to savour my own well-earned cup.

How easy it seems to go into the kitchen, turn on the electric kettle, or heat up some milk from the fridge. Everything at Amari Mandali was an adventure, even washing. Just before sunset, at the cool end of the day, I used to take my soap dish and towel and walk down to the river, being careful not to go between the buffalo calf and its mother, who glared at me fiercely. She had long, sharp horns. The water was very low in this dry season. Little streams trickled between the large expanses of rock, and I sat in one, just wider than my body, and washed. As someone might see me, I used to wear a very thin, full, blue cotton skirt, hitched under my arms so it covered my body. I had to wash and rinse myself in stages, which called for ingenuity. I would watch the sky form its peachy-coloured streamers, preparing for sunset, and hear the birds' evening call. I felt the cool breeze on my back and arms, a welcome relief after the close heat of the day. And I can't remember a time when water felt so refreshing; washing sweat and dust from my skin was immensely satisfying. I had to be out of the river before sunset, because Mira had told me that the snakes liked to swim in the water at night. I had never seen a snake here, but in the monsoon season they used to gather around the wells, making Shakuntla frightened to go and fetch water. She was the 19-year-old tribal girl who worked at Amari Mandali.

Baths in England never seem to be an adventure, to have that deeply enjoyable and exhilarating quality, the kind of experience that puts you in touch with the sheer joy and intensity of being alive. I wonder what the word 'adventure' really means. I get up and find the dictionary to look it up under the hall light. The Oxford English Dictionary, interestingly, describes an adventure as, 'Risk, danger; daring enterprise; unexpected incident; hazardous activity.' That's not what I meant about bathing in the river. There wasn't much risk involved; the exhilaration came more from it being something out of the norm, and the beauty and naturalness of the surroundings. Is there any enjoyment in 'risk, danger, hazard'? I suppose hang-gliding, parachuting and bungee-jumping have a bit more risk to them, but also careful safety regulations. Maybe people have invented these comparatively hazardous sports because our lives are generally so safe nowadays. If risk and danger were part of your everyday life, perhaps bungee-jumping would have no appeal. Women in parts of Africa have a one in five chance of dying in pregnancy or childbirth. Children in Afghanistan risk being blown up on their way to the bakery. These are not 'adventures' in my mind, though they involve risk, danger, hazard. Maybe an adventure has a degree of risk or hazard, but after a certain point a situation ceases to be an adventure for anyone.

As I think about this, I realise there's another factor: people choose to bungee jump; they don't choose to risk being blown up on the way to the bakery. I chose to go to India; I didn't choose to have something go wrong with my pregnancy and have rods the size of knitting needles stuck in me. But, on the risk scale, my life isn't in any danger, and I can rest when I need to. I am not anaemic, like so many women in the developing world, where more than half a million women die each year from pregnancy-related causes; that's one per minute. If I were a poor woman in India, I reflect, I would have gone into labour at about 30 weeks, with all the polyhydramnios. I would have given birth to a premature baby, who would probably have died immediately. Then I'd be back to work in the fields again, with little chance to recover. Women in those circumstances can't win. If they don't suffer all the risks of pregnancy and childbirth, and are childless, like Vanita, then they lose their husband and their self-esteem: for being a mother is integral to being a woman. Their lives hold little choice, few opportunities for change.

Maybe, I mused, as I am in this situation which I didn't choose, my baby's life in the balance, and more drainings looming ahead, I have realised that the thing to do is to choose it anyway. That's what we did when we created it as a project. And, strangely, there is something of the quality of washing in the river in India about this whole situation. Perhaps this is an adventure I am having. It is certainly an 'unexpected incident', and there is an element of richness about living life in this new, unknown territory. It calls me to be on the edge, reaching way beyond where I could normally reach.

My mug is empty and Cleo is curled up beside me. I turn on my side and lie down again, feeling warm and safe in my bed.

Chapter Five

Balance

*Security does not exist in Nature, nor do the
children of men as a whole experience it.
Avoiding danger is no safer in the long run
than outright exposure.
Life is either a daring adventure or nothing.*
                                    Helen Keller

Nick is painting a record cover for the singer, Sally Oldfield, and she has come around again to be drawn. She is beautiful, with big green eyes and a long, elegant nose, but she doesn't think she is attractive. So she finds it very difficult to keep still when Nick is drawing her. We are all sitting in the studio, and after a short stint of painting her, Nick is working on the picture by himself, while Sally and I sit on the carpet and talk. She is eating one of the exotic take-away salads that she always brings with her.

We talk about her boyfriends and the sources of her songs, about Alice and the project to do everything we can to help her. She tells me she has learnt Reiki, and offers to give Alice and me some healing. I don't know much about Reiki except that it works on energy levels. So I lie on the bed on my side, and she lays her hands gently on my bump. She keeps them there for a while, as I focus on breathing slowly, and visualising Alice. Then she moves them to my shoulders, my head, my legs. I feel peaceful and relaxed under her touch. She spends about 20 minutes on it, and I lie there for some time after she has finished, my body still feeling very relaxed and content, with Alice at rest inside me. Nick asks Sally to sit for him and my thoughts drift away again in the silence.

I am sitting cross-legged behind my classmate Lesley Machin, wearing my navy-blue pinafore and black gym-shoes. There is no temptation to talk in assemblies because we are sitting in order of height from the stage to the back of the hall. I hardly know the girls sitting either side of me. They are in 1C for (Cavell) or 1N (Nightingale), not 1D (Darling), like me. I'm not really listening to the reading. My mind is in Narnia, as I am in the middle of turning *Prince Caspian* into a play on my father's dark green portable typewriter. Then I hear a line: 'Live each day as if it were thy last.' I wonder about that. How would I live as if I might wake up dead the next morning?

I smile to myself, lying on my side on the carpeted floor and looking up at Sally and Nick, each focused and still. I feel so peaceful and content. It is a paradox, because in one sense there is no certainty, no stability, about the future, and therefore, apparently no peace or contentment; but the very uncertainty of the future makes me appreciate every little comfort at home with a heightened awareness. Maybe that's what was meant by 'Live each day as if it were thy last.'

Sometimes when Sally is here, but more often when she isn't, I play the album that Nick is illustrating: *The Flame*. It is all I ever want to play for weeks; I'm not sure why. The songs have a kind of nostalgic, wistful feel; but perhaps that's just the feelings I associate with them, for this beautiful lost time of being pregnant with Alice. Whenever I play the tape later, it will immediately recall those days, passing slowly by; the long periods lying on the bed, sometimes talking to friends and relatives on the phone, sometimes just thinking. Occasionally people come to see us, me sitting in state on the bed.

Every morning when I wake, I feel my abdomen to see how tight it is, and try to assess whether I need to be drained again. Wednesday comes; now I have survived another week and am still OK. On Friday I have the difficult task of deciding if I can get through the weekend without becoming too big. I decide I can. I am so conscious all the time that if I make the wrong decision, it

could mean life or death to Alice, so every decision is made slowly
and calmly. It reminds me of a passage in Peter Matthiessen's *The
Snow Leopard*. Travelling through the Himalayas, the author sees
a high narrow ledge ahead, which he knows the party will have to
travel along soon. I remember vividly his description of crawling
along the ledge on his hands and knees, terrified to look at the
enormous drop below. The porters, the B'on-pos, are just behind
him, singing and carrying huge bundles. As they reach this narrow
strip, they fall completely silent, and, staring straight ahead, they
seem to glide along, skimming between the twin dangers: of being
too close to the edge and falling over, or being too near the cliff
wall and their loads bumping them over. I am skirting between the
twin dangers of labour being set off by the draining, or going into
labour because I'm too big. What might set me off balance here is
the thought of the pain of draining. I hate needles as much as I hate
cliff edges. I go over to the bookshelf and find my copy: pale blue
paperback with a white leopard on the cover. The passage begins,

*'Between clinging and letting go, I feel a terrific struggle. This is a
fine chance to let go, to "win my life by losing it", which means not
recklessness but acceptance, not passivity but non-attachment.'*

That is where I am in this whole situation: committed to doing
everything to give Alice the best chance, but not attached to the
outcome. And what did that phrase mean, 'win my life by losing
it'?

On Monday, I know I have to be drained again, so I call Nicky.
It is December 23rd, and there is even a festive atmosphere in
the hospital, light-hearted and a bit frivolous. Nicky, Nick and I
saunter into the Harris Birthright Centre, and ask Angela for the
entonox.

'I'll have to borrow it from the labour ward,' she says, 'so can you
wait till things have quietened down a bit?'

'Sure,' we say, and sit down in the corridor. I am now a 'regular' and almost feel at home here. We drink hot chocolate, eat the usual cheese biscuits, and talk. It is strange how quickly we acquire new habits in a strange environment, creating our own security in familiarity. It is fun having Nicky here. We look at all the poor couples who are here for the first time. It feels rather daring talking normally and cheerfully when everyone else looks as if they are about to be shot.

At some point Nicky mentions another of her clients who went to the Harris Birthright Centre, with her female partner, and how kind Kypros was to them both. There is a slight pause, and Nick asks,

'How do gay women get pregnant?'

Nicky smiles.

'They usually get a male friend to donate some sperm.'

'Gay men?'

'Not necessarily. They might be. The sperm stays alive for about two hours.'

'Do you have to put it in a special container?' I ask.

'No, a jam jar or something like that,' Nicky says casually, 'and then you put it in with a teaspoon.'

'A teaspoon! And it works?'

'Well, it's as good as any other method.'

We giggle and look around to see if anyone else is listening. The corridor is now almost empty. We feel like school kids in a free period.

Eventually I am called by Worried Unsmiling Anthony. After a brief scan, he sets me up with a large cylinder of entonox. Chatting in the corridor has lessened my anxiety, but now I am in the room where I'll be drained, I start to feel shaky again. Nicky explains how to put the black rubber mask over my face and take deep breaths to activate the valve. Thank God I have the entonox!

'It takes about five breaths to really take effect, so start before he begins,' she explains.

I don't much like the idea of putting the mask over my face. It makes me think of wartime gas masks. I think it will be claustrophobic or smell of rubber. I handle it cautiously.

'And you can't take too much,' she says, 'because after a while it just drops out of your hand, and then, of course, you stop breathing it.'

I take my first breath, expecting it to be hard to breathe, like sucking air out of something, but it feels quite normal. The gas doesn't smell of anything, nor does the mask. I can hear the sound of my breathing echoing loudly inside it. And after a few breaths I start to feel wonderfully light-headed, and far less anxious. I remove the mask to tell Nicky. My speech comes out slurred and slow as if I were drunk. Amused, I start giggling. I am still wondering how much I will feel, as Antony starts getting the equipment ready. I don't look at the needle. I make sure I don't. It still hurts. I can feel, through a haze of entonox, the long metal rod stabbing through my muscles. I yell into the mask. Once the needle is in, I find I can feel it less than before, which means that the usual hour passes more easily. It makes the difference I need. I couldn't have gone through that terrifying feeling of panic again.

At last the time is up. Another two litres, so I am set up to last the week over Christmas. As I try to sit up I find that my body has registered the pain, even if my mind hasn't. It is still more than half an hour before I can actually sit up, even with help.

By now it is quite late, and we can hear a conversation in Greek in the corridor. I see two men go into the main scanning room and start making loud banging noises. Kypros wanders into our room, laughing, and calling out something to them in Greek over his shoulder. I say, 'Can I ask you a question?'

'Sure, sure,' he says, leaning against the desk.

'Well, what exactly is the connection between a diaphragmatic hernia and plueral oedema?'

'That's a good question,' he replies, looking down and pulling his beard. 'Let me think. Well, they do tend to occur together, but why, I'm not sure. It could be that the hernia inhibits the breathing movements that the baby would normally make, thus causing the oedema; but I really don't know. Yes, that's a good question...'

The banging noises in the next room get louder.

'Is that a new kind of foetal medicine next door?' asks Nick.

Kypros laughs. 'That's right: foetal surgery.' He chuckles to himself, and I think of the delicacy, the precision of all his procedures on Alice and me. 'No, they are laying white ceramic floor tiles for me.'

We are unable to go to Sheffield to stay with my family at Christmas, as it is too far from London. I need to be within an hour of King's, so my aunt Priscilla offers us her house in Woking, while she goes to stay with her son and daughter-in-law in Cardiff. Veronica is a midwife and on call over Christmas. We catch the train on Christmas Eve, and settle ourselves in.

We spend Christmas in a little cocoon. We curl up on the sofa, with a rug, and read, and watch TV. We hardly ever watch it usually, so it is a treat. And every now and then Nick prepares some of the delicious food that Priscilla has left for us. We have two books of babies' names, and look through them, searching for a middle name for Alice. But nothing seems to fit, and in the end we decide she must just be called Alice.

On Christmas day we phone our families, mine in Sheffield, Nick's in the British Virgin Islands, and unwrap our presents. Nick has given me a lovely golden box, with lots of different things inside, including a bendy black hairband from The Body Shop, some Mamatoto Baby lotion and Baby Aloe, the new Enya tape and little soaps.

We watch a film about a kind of modern Scrooge. There is a little boy who hasn't spoken at all for years, since his father died. I really feel for this child, alone in his frozen grief. The Scrooge character goes through all sorts of weird and wonderful eye-opening experiences and starts, of course, to become a nicer, more generous person. And at the end the little boy comes up and smiles, and says something to him. It is too much. I turn to Nick and cry and cry on his shoulder. I can't even articulate what it has to do with Alice, but something has gone right through to me. The boy was so vulnerable and closed down; his speaking was like a miracle. Perhaps I want a miracle for Alice.

'You know, I am remembering my times in India and with The Hunger Project much more at the moment,' I tell Nick.

'Why is that, do you think?' he asks.

'I'm not sure. I keep feeling aware of how lucky I am to know I'm safe, at least, and that Alice is having everything done for her. But it's more than just that. I think there are similarities. Being in an unfamiliar situation that means I have to find new resources in myself reminds me of India, and the focusing on a difficult and important goal reminds me of The Hunger Project.'

'Yes, it's something about living life at the edge. You remind me of how you were in the enrolment campaign, but even stronger and more centred.'

I suppose that campaign did take strength, but I was so passionately committed to the end of hunger in the world, that the experience was exhilarating. We asked person after person to sign a card as an expression of their commitment to the end of hunger, and engaged them in a conversation so they could see that they made a difference to creating a wordwide commitment. I remember keeping my teams inspired, sometimes up to midnight, buying cups of take-away tea or cream cheese bagels, and then making a promise for the next half-hour, our bodies longing just to go home and sleep. To create the end of hunger in a climate of resignation and lack of knowledge was a huge undertaking, but it was what The Hunger Project was committed to. This enormous, growing movement all over the world was starting to cause a paradigm shift. And a big promise like causing the end of hunger in the world is only reached through the keeping of thousands and thousands of smaller promises.

With Alice there is even more at stake, because breaking the promise to keep her inside my body would almost certainly mean the end. But there is also less at stake. Our promise then was so enormous; to end the 18 million deaths a year caused by malnutrition. Here there's a direct connection: one baby, my baby, that I have to do my best to keep alive. Out in Leicester Square, with stacks of enrolment cards and a folding table, we had to keep reminding ourselves of the interconnectedness of the world, and the greater promise divided into much smaller ones, or there could have seemed no connection at all. What else but a promise would have one go up to stranger after stranger with a clipboard and ask them, 'Would you like to sign a card for the end of hunger?'

It seems so strange now, what we did, but I knew then that what was missing to end hunger was the global commitment. In 1985, no one could have foreseen the World Summit for Children, five years ahead, nor the creation of Hunger-Free Zones all over India, the Indian Government's co-operation with the Indian Hunger Project, which was acting as a catalyst to bring the right groups of people together. In fact, maybe those things happened because of literally millions of conversations which took place all over the world, for several years, slowly dispelling the myths and altering the cultural awareness concerning the issues of hunger. Throughout that time, the emphasis was always that the 'individual is the key', because it is only in individuals, not organisations, that commitment can be generated. I, myself, had over 10,000 conversations in two years, and watched the climate of thought change. People's answer to my question was always the very thing that was stopping them from taking action, or making them shut the problem out of their minds.

'Why do they have so many children when they know they are

going to die?' asks a woman, coming out of the shopping precinct carrying heavy bags from Sainsbury's. She sounds frustrated and powerless, not expecting an answer to her rhetorical question, unaware that she is repeating what I hear so many people say every day.

'You're thinking of the pictures you've seen on telly, of the famine victims, aren't you?' I ask.

'Yes, it's terrible, you see those little children, covered in flies, just lying there, like little old men. I can hardly bear to watch it.'

She sounds upset and angry, the voice of helplessness and confusion.

'Well, the famine only hit them a few months ago,' I reply gently. 'When they had their children they were still farming their fields and there was just enough to feed them.'

'But why do they have so many? You shouldn't have so many children if you can't afford them.' Here is the next layer, just below the first. Now I can hear the voice of the tabloids, the 'everybody knows' stuff.

'They have so many children because so many die before they reach adulthood, because of their poor nutrition and lack of medical care. They haven't got any pensions in Africa; they need children to look after them in old age. It hurts them just as much as us to see their children die, but they have no choice. When women see their children are living, they stop having so many.'

I go on, because I can see she is listening. 'Do you know, 84 countries have ended hunger since the beginning of this century, and in every case, the birth rate has gone right down within 10 years. Look at how many children our grandparents used to have.'

'Yes, that's true; my grandmother had six brothers and sisters.' The layers of the onion are peeling off, layers that may have stayed there if it hadn't been for a chance conversation like this with a stranger. Her voice is calmer now.

'But what can we do? I've sent money, but you still see them on the news, don't you?'

'Well, what's needed is a global commitment to ending hunger for good, not just patching up things till they break down again. And the only way a world-wide commitment can be created is by individual people being committed to it happening. You could sign one of these cards committing yourself to "making the end of hunger and starvation by the end of the century an idea whose time has come".'

'Yeah, I'll sign one of them.'

As she fills it in, I continue.

'There are now five million people around the world who have expressed commitment to the end of hunger, and that's powerful. And you can tell other people the facts, and that what is missing in the world is the global commitment.'

'Can I take a couple of those cards? I could ask my daughter and my husband to sign one.' She says goodbye and I turn to the next passer-by. 'Excuse me…'

And so it went on. One rarely knew, with people in the street, how those conversations and their signing a card pledging their commitment altered their actions or conversations in the future, but there clearly was a shift in the wind; a critical mass was reached. During this time, over Christmas, I often think about one extraordinary conversation.

It is about eleven at night in Leicester Square, and I approach a man who looks Indian; he has fine features and dark rings under his eyes.

'Excuse me; would you like to…'

'What's this?' He turns to me sharply, seeing the picture of African people on the front of the pamphlet I am holding. 'Who are you?'

'I'm from The Hunger Project.'

'Look at these people in your photographs!' he seethes. 'What right have you to show African people? How can you speak for them?' He glares at me. 'You white people, you come out and tell Africans what to do… Who is behind this organisation? Tell me.'

He's a journalist, I think. It is September 1986, three months after a horribly damning article about us on the front page of *The Sunday Times*. All the trustees have put their houses on the line to sue the paper, collecting vast quantities of data to clear The Hunger Project's name. They later settle out of court, and *The Times* makes a small mention of the full-scale retraction. But at that moment I am scared.

'Is it American?' he persists, in the same angry tone. Well, if he is going to write a story anyway, I'll give him all the truth I can cram in. Maybe I'll convince him. The challenge is on, and I can feel my heart beating fast.

'It started in the States, but it exists now all over the world – '

'Who's behind it then, the CIA?'

I look steadily at him. Explaining isn't getting anywhere. 'You tell me,' I say. 'You've already made up your mind. There's nothing I can say that will make any difference, because you've already decided, even though you know nothing about us. You think we don't listen to black people, but you're not listening to me.'

He stops, for the first time. Touché.

'OK, OK, I'll listen,' he says, grudgingly.

'Well, it's funded by individuals only, not governments or churches, all over the world, in Europe, Africa, India, America. It's a grass-roots organisation, run in each country by the people themselves. We are working in partnership with the people of Africa. We don't tell people what to do; that is one of the reasons why hunger persists. We need to give people the opportunities to end their own hunger, to empower them to be free from the cycle of poverty. So we show people looking happy, like this, in contrast to all the famine pictures that make people give out of pity. It insults people to be given to out of pity. They need partnership and opportunities, not pity.'

I am sounding clear and calm, but my passion is coming through. He is starting to listen. I am still being interrogated, though.

'Have you been to Africa?'

He gives me the kind of piercing look that makes it impossible to lie, even if I'd wanted to.

'No, but I've worked in India, among tribal women on a small-scale project run by Indian people. The co-ordinators asked the women what they needed to earn some income. The women decided to start a buffalo-milk co-operative and a carpet co-operative.'

'And what were you doing there?'

'I made notes, and wrote reports, and set up a small charity here, in England, which sent out funds to them, and found Gujarati workers to train people in running a health clinic, and in buffalo husbandry.'

His voice starts to change.

'I'm sorry,' he said, 'I have to be suspicious. You know, I never heard of The Hunger Project before.'

'Where are you from?' I ask.

'South Africa. I've been here for an ANC conference. What are you doing in Leicester Square, then?'

'We're asking people to sign cards expressing their commitment to the end of hunger and to take action in their own way. I made a promise that we would have 70,000 people in Britain sign these cards in two months, and this campaign is going on in 21 other countries at the same time. I work about 16 hours a day at the moment. But I'm determined we're going to do it. I can't forget that children are dying of hunger every day.'

He can obviously hear my commitment in the way I speak, because he starts looking at me with interest.

'Would you carry a gun? Would you kill anyone, to reach your goal?'

'No,' I reply, surprised at the question.

'You wouldn't ever kill anyone for your cause?'

'No,' I answer, realising that his strange question came from his experience in South Africa, where guns were part of everyday life.

'That's very good,' he says, looking thoughtful, and his voice softens. 'You know, I spent three years in jail on Robben Island. I used to play chess with Nelson Mandela. He's a remarkable man. But how can I not carry a gun?' He turns to me again, his voice showing his controlled desperation. 'You know what they did? They killed my mother, and my father, and then they took my girlfriend. They sent me her fingernails in an envelope. I admire anyone who can say they won't use violence, but – what's the matter?'

The tears are pouring uncontrollably down my face.

'Why are you crying?' he asks, anxiously, taking my hand and rubbing it.

'For you, for what you've suffered,' I say, trying unsuccessfully to wipe my tears away with the other hand.

'But you mustn't cry! These are my problems, not yours. This is amazing; you don't even know me.'

'I know, but you're a human being like me. And they are my problems too; we all share the world. I want the world to work for everyone.'

'But you are doing such great work here; you must focus on what good you are doing.'

It is impossible to believe that five minutes ago I thought he was a bigot, out to destroy The Hunger Project. We had both got each other wrong. The tears go on, and he seems so touched and concerned.

'You are a really good person, you know. I'm sorry I was so angry before. I didn't realise...'

'That's all right, really...' I manage to stop the tears and attempt a smile.

'You are rare, you know. You have a big heart.' I think for a moment he is going to cry. 'Look, give me one of those cards. Yes, and a pamphlet. I'm afraid I must go. My friends are waiting for me and you have a target to make.' He smiles. 'But, look, if ever The Hunger Project needs the ANC, we'll be there!' and with a final squeeze of my hand, he is off, leaving me raw and alive in the summer evening.

I wonder if he ever remembered that conversation? Nine years later, The Hunger Project award President Mandela the Africa Prize for Leadership for the Sustainable End of Hunger. The Prize is awarded annually to a leader in Africa who has made a significant difference to the end of hunger on a national, regional or continental level. It is renowned in Africa as the African Nobel Peace Prize. This particular ceremony achieves international press coverage, showing President Mandela on stage with President Clinton. What a change from the constant vigil outside the South African embassy, and the banners saying 'Free Nelson Mandela'. Who knows what conversations altered the climate of thinking about him?

And here I am, lying in bed in Woking at Christmas. We have just gone to bed when I notice I am getting slight contractions. I am alarmed. After all, I've done so well so far, not going into labour. But maybe my body has had enough.

'Perhaps they're just false contractions, practice ones – what are they called?' says Nick.

'Braxton Hicks. I don't know. This is the first time I've had anything like this. But I've got a slight pain in the bottom of my back, too, a bit like a period pain.'

Nick watches me, concerned, as I time the gaps. They seem to be happening regularly every five minutes.

'Is there anything I can do?'

'No, thanks, darling, there's nothing to do yet.'

Nick puts his arms around me and we just lie there for a while, similar scenarios running through our minds of rushing to a strange hospital in Woking, or Guildford, people not knowing how to deal with Alice's problems, and no Nicky or Katrina.

'Anyway, I have to keep her in for another two or three weeks, to give her lungs a chance to grow.'

'Didn't Douglas say that a baby's lungs are fully developed at 34 weeks?'

'A normal baby, yes, but maybe Alice's will go on growing. They said 36 or 37 weeks was the minimum. She'll just be stronger anyway. She needs every chance she can get.'

'Yes.'

After a while, I say, 'Well, the contractions aren't getting any stronger. Why don't you go to sleep, and I'll just do some deep breathing.'

'Are you sure? You don't want me to get you a drink or anything?'

'No, thanks. I'll be all right.'

So I lie in the dark, breathing regularly and slowly, concentrating my mind on relaxing the muscles, calming the uterus down. It seems to go on a long time; these slight contractions, my mind wandering off, then returning to focus on my breathing and the sensations in my body. They aren't lessening at all. After all, I think, labour can last ages. Maybe it feels just like this for some hours. But I won't do anything unless they increase. I don't want to go to hospital, even for a false alarm. This bed is the best place to be.

Thoughts keep coming, unasked, into my mind. What if she dies? What if she dies because these few missing weeks mean that she can't quite pull through? I've got to stop the contractions.

But they continue, as Nick lies asleep beside me. I press the little light inside the clock. One o'clock. At least they aren't getting any worse. I know it's possible. I can stop them. We've got far more control than we realise. I go on with the deep breathing, unable to sleep, my mind following thoughts, then returning, my body alert. I wish this wasn't happening. I just want to sleep, but I know I mustn't. Left to themselves, the contractions might increase. My willpower seems like my only power. It reminds me of The Hunger Project enrolment campaigns, late at night in Leicester Square, going on till we made our day's target.

Eventually, after about two hours of breathing steadily, I begin to feel I am winning, and my body feels more relaxed. My mind starts drifting, and I fall asleep. In the morning the contractions have stopped, but I feel sure that it wasn't chance. Another hurdle over. I feel as if my willpower and intention is being tested constantly, from perpetually unexpected directions, tested to see if I can really have my baby live.

December 31st 1991. I am getting large and tight again, so I go for my fourth draining on New Year's Eve. We are getting almost blasé about it all.

'You only come here for the entonox, don't you?' remarks Douglas as he fastens me up for another siphoning session. There is a decidedly festive feel in the ward.

'Are you going to a party tonight?' I ask.

'Oh, we'll probably go to the Phoenix and Firkin for a bit.'

This is the wonderful old pub across the road that is part of Denmark Hill Railway Station, with bare floorboards and log fires. Another 2.6 litres later, I am slimmer again. I feel rather like a concertina. How my poor uterus puts up with it I don't know. I notice that the fluid is building up faster than before, so as Douglas throws away the dressings and says I can go, I ask, 'Aren't you going to scan me?'

'OK, if you want me to,' he says and takes us into the main scanning room.

'Hmm,' he says, after a while, 'the pleural oedema has increased a bit.'

He shows us the area inside her left lung. The black line has thickened.

'Is there anything that can be done?' I ask, worried by this new development.

'Yes,' says Douglas calmly, 'we can insert a 'shunt' to drain it back into the amniotic fluid and give her lungs more room. I'll discuss it with Kypros, so can you come back on Friday?'

'OK,' I say, and remark to Nick on the way out how just when I seem to get the slightest bit complacent about anything, something unexpected always happens. 'It's as if the universe is saying, "Right, you've handled that test successfully. Let's see what you make of this next one!"'

⌣‿⟩

January 3rd 1992. We aren't absolutely sure they are going to put a 'shunt' into her, so I don't allow myself to think about it too much. I lie on my side along a row of chairs in the corridor and try to sleep. When Angela trundles by with an entonox trolley, I ask, 'Is that for me?'

She calls back over her shoulder, 'Yes, it is, Chrissy.'

'Oh, good,' I say. I am feeling quite anticipatory. How different from a month ago! I put my hand on my abdomen, shut my eyes and breathe deeply.

At last we are called to the usual scanning room. I notice there is now a little brass plate on the door saying, 'Hippocrates Room'. Inside, the white ceramic floor tiles give an incongruously Mediterranean feel to the room. It reminds me of a hotel in a Greek holiday resort. Kypros is seated at the scanner, Angela at the computer and Ruth preparing things on a trolley. I don't look at the trolley. Kypros is in a joking mood already, pretending to squirt the 'jelly' on my tummy before I've even pulled back my clothes. Then on the screen he shows us the 'black' fluid around Alice's right lung, which seems to be compressing it even more. At this point, not knowing seems slightly worse than knowing, so I ask how the shunt would get in, and Douglas says, 'Down a needle.'

'They must be tiny,' I remark, trying to sound light.

'Yes, they are.'

'I also need to be drained,' I tell them.

'Ah, so we can use the same needle, can't we?' Kypros realises.

It all seems to be happening quickly, luckily. Not too much

waiting. Kypros makes some remark about my not needing entonox because I'll faint. Does he mean the entonox will make me faint? Is he making a joke? I don't get what the joke is, anyway. I am desperate to make sure I have the entonox. I don't want to take any chances.

'I only faint from pain, not from entonox,' I reply.

'It's quite good to faint with this stuff,' Douglas replies, and I realise I am going to have it, thank God. I ask Nick to remove two of the pillows. This means I can see more of the ceiling and less of the action.

'What do you do, Nick?' asks Kypros, still staring at the screen.

'I'm an artist.'

'You do paintings, or what?'

'Yes, oil paintings, mostly. I had three exhibitions in the Caribbean, where my parents live.'

'He's a brilliant artist,' I say, confidently.

'Really?' says Kypros, looking at me carefully. 'Do other people say this, or just his wife?'

'Well, yes, quite a few other people have,' says Nick – modest but always truthful.

Ruth hands me the entonox mask, and I hold on to Nick's hand tightly with my left hand, and put the mask over my face with my right. The moment is getting nearer.

'I'm pretty nervous,' I say.

'No, you're not,' says Kypros, with apparent indignation. 'What have you got to be nervous about?'

'Well, it's new, isn't it?' I say, trying to put into words what is obvious. 'It's the Unknown.'

'No, it's not new; I've done it once before!' Kypros replies, obviously delighting in his own joke. 'Anyway, I've read the book. A pity it was in Spanish, but there were some good diagrams.'

Douglas is grinning.

'And you've seen the film,' says Ruth.

'And you've got the T-shirt,' I add, and breathe in more entonox.

I am considerably less nervous now, but still in that anticipatory state before the needle actually goes in.

I am concentrating on the ceiling, Nick is watching the screen, and Douglas is preparing a file on the computer. I hear some slight giggles, and Nick tells me that Kypros is squirting some of the local anaesthetic at Douglas from a syringe. I am beginning to feel a kind of alert calm, but I want to have people talking.

'Keep talking,' I say urgently.

'Er...' says Nick.

I feel the pinprick of the local anaesthetic.

'Now, there's going to be a slight pressure,' says Kypros. I look hard at the ceiling, thankful for the light floaty feeling of the entonox.

'Keep breathing in, darling: deep breaths,' Angela says.

I don't feel it too much, though Nick says later it looks more like a size 20 knitting needle this time. Even bigger than the draining needle.

'You're going to be a real expert with this entonox by the time it comes to labour, aren't you, Chrissy?' remarks Ruth. 'Maybe you should have piped entonox, Kypros, as well as piped music.' I guess they have been joking earlier about getting piped music.

'Sally Oldfield,' I say, into the mask, knowing Nick will hear me.

'What did she say?' asks Kypros, still looking at the screen.

'Sally Oldfield,' said Nick.

'Who's Sally Oldfield?' asked Ruth.

'Mike Oldfield's sister,' Nick said. Kypros is moving the scan around; searching for the right spot on Alice's ribcage, I think. 'Her music's very different, though. She's a star in Germany, and she's asked me to design a record cover for her new album. So I'm going to be famous,' he adds. Kypros grunts. He is half listening. 'Who's this?' he asks.

'Sally Oldfield,' Ruth replies. 'Mike Oldfield's sister.'

'And they're using your painting?'

'Well, I haven't finished it yet. But she's asked me to paint one, yes.'

I stare intently at the stretch marks on the polystyrene ceiling, listening to every word, completely aware of Kypros's search inside my abdomen, and hearing the familiar sound of my own breath into the mask. The thought passes through my mind that I've never been more alive than at this moment, with every ounce of my being present and alert, focusing all my intention on my little Alice, sending her love and reassurance.

'Is she good-looking?' asks Douglas.

'Oh, yes,' says Nick, and I nod.

'What does she look like?' asks Ruth.

'Does she fancy you?' asks Douglas.

'Oh, yes,' says Nick, teasingly.

'Do you fancy her?'

'Oh, yes.'

'Are you listening to this?' Kypros asks me.

I nod, feeling a delightful lightness in this wonderfully absurd conversation.

'What's Mike Oldfield like?' says Angela. 'Is he good-looking?'

'Well, I suppose so,' says Nick. I nod vigorously.

'Well, Chrissy thinks so. Do you fancy him, Chrissy?'

I nod again. Then I feel a little 'ping'. I think I hear it, but I guess it just travels through my body.

'That was it,' I say into the mask. There is a lull as everyone watches the screen.

'Keep talking,' I say quickly, outside the mask.

'Right, well she's about medium height, fair hair,' begins Nick.

'Who's this?' asks Kypros.

'We're on Sally Oldfield still,' explains Ruth. Everyone is now intently watching the screen. I feel like a football pitch on which a great match is being played, unable to see the game. I am waiting for another 'ping', another goal to be scored. But there isn't one. Instead, Kypros says, 'Look, look at this!'

'Look, darling!' says Nick, sounding excited, so I raise my head to look at the screen.

'See?' says Kypros. We can see one of her little round lungs, and the tiny shunt, with the fluid draining from inside her chest cavity into my amniotic fluid. There it is on the screen, and the pleural oedema is disappearing before our eyes.

'Isn't that amazing?' says Nick.

'I'd say your chances are more like 70% now,' says Kypros. I feel so excited. It's working!

'Can you take this, Angela?' I hear him ask, apparently extricating something. 'Now, you're about to make a mess,' he says. 'Yes, you are! See?' There is obviously some more fun going on, and I guess the 'operation' part is over. I can just see some water coming out of the top of a fine tube somewhere above my abdomen, and feel something wet and warm on my tummy.

'Honestly, these patients are ungrateful,' Kypros goes on, getting into full swing. 'I do all these things for them and what do they do? Squirt their amniotic fluid all over me, my new tie, my new underpants…'

'Kypros, honestly!' says Angela.

By this time I am giggling helplessly. 'Is this my jokes or the entonox?' he asks. I'm not sure myself; the entonox seems to have run out, but I'm not really in pain. I keep the mask on anyway, at least to keep my breathing rhythmic.

Suddenly Kypros says, 'Turn on your side,' and starts to pull me over like a beached whale. I hear the loud pouring of amniotic fluid into a basin as they adjust things. It hurts a bit, so I moan into the mask.

'It's all right, Chrissy, there's nothing wrong,' says Ruth.

'I'm not worried,' I say, which is true.

'She's just making cat noises,' explains Nick.

There is a fine fountain of amniotic fluid coming out of the tube in my abdomen, like water out of a stone cherub's mouth, landing two feet below in a yellow plastic washing-up bowl on the floor.

Kypros is guiding its direction with one hand.

'If anyone comes through the door and sees this,' remarks Kypros, 'they'll think I'm peeing into this bowl.'

Angela bends down to pick up the bowl while Douglas replaces it with another. I hear my amniotic fluid being poured down the sink.

'Look, you've spilt some,' says Ruth, getting a mop and cleaning the floor round Kypros's feet. I am having fun, in a strange kind of way. I keep making noises into the mask to relieve the aching pain round the needle.

'Who is this patient?' asks Kypros. 'She says 'Keep talking', she makes pre-orgasmic noises...'

'Oh, women always do that when they're using entonox,' says Ruth. 'It's quite usual. Isn't Kypros wonderful?' she says to me sweetly.

'Yes, definitely,' I say. 'Cyprus,' I add, translating it to English.

'Actually, my name isn't really Kypros, it's Kyprianos, after St Cyprian, but when I came to England I changed it to Kypros. I didn't want people calling me Anus or something.'

'Are you Scottish or Swedish, Douglas?' I ask.

'I'm English,' says Douglas firmly. This obviously isn't the first time he's been asked.

'He came over with the Vikings,' remarks Kypros. 'How long ago was that?'

'700 AD roughly,' I say.

'700 AD...' says Kypros. 'He doesn't look that old, does he?'

'Are you a teacher, Chrissy?' asks Ruth.

'I used to be. I taught English and Drama.'

'Actually, you know,' says Nick, 'she's an Oxford scholar. She doesn't often tell people this. Chrissy knows about lots of things.'

'I thought she looked a bit odd,' says Kypros.

'Just because you didn't get in,' Angela remarks.

'I didn't apply.'

'Where did you go?' I ask.

'St Thomas's, University of London. You're meant to be breathing that entonox, aren't you?'

'Oh, the entonox ran out ages ago.'

'Oh, in that case, I won't take any more off you. I was going to take off lots more, but...'

I know he is joking. The room already seems like a kindergarten in summer when children have been sailing boats in plastic basins. Ruth is busy mopping up.

'How much was that, Douglas?' Kypros asks.

'About 3 litres,' replies Douglas with a slight giggle. 'Well nearer to 3 than 2.'

So much for all that accurate measuring.

I remember, as I am sitting in the corridor recovering, that I want Kypros to put in writing my preferences about the birth, so I ask Angela if I can ask him a few questions. We wait a while and, as the patients gradually leave, he comes along. He is in high spirits.

'I want to ask you some questions,' I tell him.

'How many?' he asks.

'Four,' I say, making up a number.

'Well, you're only allowed two. Go ahead.'

'Is she still breech?' I ask, as a preliminary.

'Yes. That's it. That's one question you've wasted. You need to do better than that.'

I grin, and try to think straight.

'Well, if she stays breech, is there any need for me to have a Caesarean, or can I give birth naturally?'

'The only thing that matters is that the paediatricians are there as the baby is born. You can give birth standing on your head, if you want.'

Chapter Six

Induction

Women reported that their memories [of childbirth 15-29 years before] were vivid and deeply felt. Those with highest long-term satisfaction ratings thought that they accomplished something important, that they were in control, and that the birth experience contributed to their self-confidence and their self-esteem. They had positive memories of their doctors' and nurses' words and actions. These positive associations were not reported among women with low satisfaction ratings.

> *Just Another Day In a Woman's Life?*
> *Women's Long-term Perceptions of*
> *Their First Birth Experience.*
> *Penny Simpkin*
> *December 1991*

January 7th 1992. On Tuesday I become aware that I can't feel Alice moving. But then, I can't remember feeling her moving much for a long time, really; the polyhydramnios has made it difficult, even when I've seen her moving on the screen. Anyway, I heard her heart beat normally yesterday when Katrina was here. But I phone Nicky, who suggests I go straight away to the Harris Birthright Centre to have a CTG.

'What's that?' I ask.

'It draws the baby's heart-beat on a graph. You must've seen the machine in the room where you're drained.'

It is five-thirty by the time we arrive, and, surprisingly, only Kypros seems to be around, finishing off. He looks serious when I say Alice isn't moving, despite the check-up on Monday, and hurries me into the scan room. He turns up the sound on the scanner, and within a few seconds we can hear the familiar little thumping sound.

'There you are,' says Kypros, wiping the jelly off my tummy with a paper towel.

'Is that it?' I ask, getting up.

'What else do you want – spaghetti?'

He is patently relieved.

'Can you show us how a shunt works?' asks Nick. Kypros grabs a piece of paper and scribbles some lines. 'This is the chest wall, and the pleural oedema, see? And the shunt – it's a tiny piece of hollow tubing, see? – goes in here and curls up at one end' – he scribbles a tight coil – 'and it curls on the outside' – scribbling another – 'so the fluid can get out but the shunt is secure.'

'Ingenious,' I say, trying to imagine how tiny these small pieces of plastic are – inside Alice, inside me. And does it hurt Alice as much as the needles do me? Or more? I don't want to think about that.

'And next time you don't feel the baby move,' he says sternly as he is going, 'don't wait till Wednesday to come in.'

'Kypros, it's Tuesday.'

He turns to me for a second and his face changes.

'Oh yes,' he grins, and is off.

From now on, I lie down for 20 minutes every day and make a mark on a piece of paper each time I feel Alice move. Little, tiny fish movements. She'll be a good swimmer, I think, after living in all this water.

January 10th 1992. I get on the scanning table and pull my top up and my trousers down, to reveal my big rounded abdomen.

Douglas turns to squirt the sticky stuff on me, and stops as he notices something.

'What's this?'

He starts peering closely at my bump. Angela and Ruth come to see what he is looking at. By each little scab or scar from the needles is written a name and a date. 'Douglas, 31/12/91; Anthony, 23/12/91.'

'I like to keep careful records,' I remark.

Douglas grins, as he reads them all out.

'How did you do it?' asks Angela.

'Biro. Nick wrote them on for me.'

'Oh, we must show them to Kypros when he comes in.'

Soon Douglas shows us the screen. The shunt in her right side seems to have worked, but there is now a build-up of pleural oedema around her left lung. I start to feel uneasy, but don't let my thoughts surface.

By the time Douglas fetches Kypros to look at the screen, the writing is either blurred or rubbed off, so Nick, knowing the importance of keeping me diverted and laughing, leans forward and pretends to sound surprised.

'What's this? Look, there's writing on her!'

I can see Kypros trying not to smile as he tries to decipher it. He points to the scar labelled 'Douglas 31/12/91'.

'Look at this!' he says. 'What were you doing putting the needle there!?'

'It was the best place to avoid the baby,' Douglas says in defence. 'And look at yours,' he adds. 'It's twice as big as mine! That'll leave a huge scar.'

'Well, Anthony's are the worst!' says Kypros.

'Oh, definitely,' Douglas agrees. Then he shows Kypros the screen, and I lie looking at the ceiling.

'Well, I think Chrissy is showing too many Right Wing tendencies,' Kypros says at last, indicating the fact that all the holes are on my right side. 'I think we need to balance out her politics with some

Trotskyist activity over here.'

Then I realise what he is talking about. They are going to put in another pleural shunt. My body starts to shake, and my heart beats faster. I'm not thinking. There are just physical sensations and a sense of dread. I haven't realised till now quite how traumatising the whole experience was last time. I ask for the entonox.

'Sorry,' says Douglas, still in a joking mood. 'There's no entonox, only ether and a hanky.' He and Angela continue their preparations. 'It always works in the films,' he adds. But I'm not in the mood for a joke. I don't relax till the now familiar mask is over my face and I am anaesthetising my fears with large doses of entonox. Knowing what is about to happen doesn't make it any easier, and, despite the entonox, I notice how alert my whole being is, waiting for it to be over. Luckily, Angela asks Nick how we met, so he tells the story, interspersed with 'Aaah, how sweet!' from Angela, and weird comments from Kypros whenever he is listening.

'... So she phoned me up and invited me out to dinner...'

'Who? Sally Oldfield?'

'No, Kypros – Chrissy. Nick's telling us how they met.'

'... And she took me to The Olive Tree in Leicester Square, and afterwards, when we kissed, loads of fireworks went off...'

'You were both drunk, weren't you? You were hallucinating. Are you sure you were in Leicester Square...?'

Then another two litres are drained off me, this time without turning me on my side, so it drains more slowly. I can't see exactly what is going on but I hear Ruth ask Kypros if he liked playing with water when he was a little boy. Finally, as he wipes down my tummy, he says, 'You need to eat a lot of protein at the moment, to make up for what you're losing in the amniotic fluid.'

It passes through my mind that I might have had more energy if I had been told that before I had lost nearly 13 litres of amniotic fluid. It never occurred to me that this fluid which just looked like pee might be full of nutrients. But the important thing is the future. I eat about a pound and a half of cheese over the next two days and feel a lot better.

In fact, I feel well enough to go to Peter's birthday party on January 15th. Nick is busy so I go by myself in a taxi. Emil is playing on the floor and Sara is breast-feeding Rosa. This is the room in which she gave birth, and now I am about to give birth. It certainly doesn't fit the pictures I had on November 5th, but that doesn't bother me. I am very proud of my enormous bump and my imminent motherhood. The only photos I have taken of me pregnant are at this party. In all of them I am smiling radiantly. There is that beautiful, peaceful bloom that you see in the faces of heavily pregnant women.

January 16th 1992. On Thursday I know I have to be drained again. My tummy is tight. I have hardly felt Alice move all week, but know somehow that she is still alive.

Douglas scans me and we notice that there is pleural effusion round both lungs again, despite the presence of the shunts. Alice doesn't seem to be moving at all. Angela tells us that Kypros will want to see us, so would we like to wait in the midwives' room? We sit on the little blue two-seater sofa and hold hands. There isn't much to say. We drink hot chocolate, eat cheese biscuits, and wait. Hour after hour goes by, and every now and then Angela pops in, looking sympathetic, and asks how we are. In answer to my questions about what is happening, she keeps saying that Kypros is really busy, but later she tells me he hates giving bad news to anyone, so he put off seeing us.

Eventually we go back into the scan room and I lie on the table. He taps my side a few times and shows Douglas the screen. Each time, you can see Alice's arm move floppily, like a rag doll. She is just lying there, alive but still.

'What does it say about Arthrogryposis?' Kypros asks, as Douglas pores over a big book from the hospital library. Douglas reads out a list of symptoms.

'You see, that doesn't really look like talipes*,' says Kypros,

---

* *Club foot*

focusing on Alice's feet, 'but I can't be sure.'

He turns to me.

'We're going to induce you tomorrow,' he says. 'We need to get this baby out now.'

'It's not quite 38 weeks yet,' I say.

'That's OK. By 37 weeks the lungs have developed as much as they will, so it is counted as full term. But just to give the baby the best possible chance, I'm going to drain the fluid from round her lungs now.'

More entonox, and two fine needle holes. I feel almost blasé about it compared to the unknown ahead. This is it. D-Day. Now I am heading rapidly towards that experience I've been wondering about for years. I think of the number of times I have heard people say, 'You can't describe childbirth to someone who hasn't been through it.'

'What do I have to do tomorrow?'

'Angela will tell you all that. Be here at eight tomorrow morning. And have sex tonight,' he adds as he walks out.

'It can set off labour,' explains Angela, smiling mischievously. 'Take her out for a hot curry tonight Nick, too, or buy her some pineapple.'

I go off to the loo. On the way back down the corridor we see Kypros, Angela, Ruth and Douglas sitting in the midwives' room drinking champagne, obviously celebrating something. I guess what it is when we arrive home and I see the headline on the newspaper: 'Saved – when she was two inches tall.' There is a photograph of a rather dazed-looking but sweet little baby, with black rings under her eyes and a little tube taped to one nostril, held by her mother, who appears as an out-of-focus profile. The caption reads, 'Natalie Robertson and her mother Susan – compatible after all, thanks to a medical breakthrough that will bring hope to thousands of women.' A little line drawing of an embryo, about 2 inches long, has a caption, 'Actual size of foetus when transfusions began.'

Susan has a rare condition called thrombocytopoenia, which

means that her body produces antibodies against her own baby's platelets, the blood component that helps clotting. She had already had one stillbirth and two terminations before Kypros tried a new technique, injecting Natalie from 11 weeks with antibodies to 'block' her own mother's immune system.

'With Natalie, the umbilical cord was too narrow to admit a tranfusion needle; instead, the donor antibodies went into her abdominal cavity. The baby's abdomen was at first smaller than the surgeon's thumbnail and any of the 25 transfusions she received could have meant miscarriage. The idea was untested – 'pure theory', says Dr Kypros Nicolaides of King's Harris Birthright Centre. 'But I think the baby's chances would have been zero without this intervention. We had to try.'

I don't sleep much that night, and feel pretty tired when Nicky picks us up at a time when I am usually still asleep. I have a bag containing night-things and lots of food and drink. I have heard about so many home births where people nibble and drink things in between contractions and the room is lit by candlelight. Like a party. So we are feeling almost excited when we arrive in the labour room. It doesn't fit my pictures of a hospital room at all. Nick says it is like a hotel. The walls have been recently rag-rolled in pastel colours with a tasteful, patterned frieze round the edge. The curtains are attractive, and are the right length for the windows. There is a bed with crisp white sheets and a white cellular blanket, an armchair and a bedside cabinet. I am really impressed by the high-backed armchair.

'Is it leather?' I ask.

'No, it's plastic,' says Nicky. 'But it's pretty comfortable. It makes it look a bit more homely and less clinical, doesn't it?'

Perhaps the best bit is the en-suite bathroom, which you have to share with the adjacent room, admittedly, but there are locks on both doors. We settle down and eat dried apricots and ask each other what we want from Room Service. Soon Ruth pops down to join the party.

'Did you have a curry last night?' she asks.

'No, but we had some pineapple,' I say. 'And sex. It didn't work.'

Although we have arrived on time, it is an hour before anyone apart from the hospital nurses comes to see us. The atmosphere in our hotel room is quite jovial by the time the double doors open and a mousy-haired man with glasses enters, followed by a small retinue of earnest-looking underlings. They seem taller than him, conscious of the power their crisp new white coats give them, but tangibly aware of their position in the hierarchy. Nick and I look alert, feeling that something is about to happen at last. Dr Stott*, the obstetric consultant, introduces himself and explains politely that he has come to palpate my abdomen and give me a scan. He presses my abdomen in various places as the underlings wheel over a small-screened scanner from the corner of the room and plug it in. A squirt of jelly, then they stare seriously at the screen as Dr Stott points out various items of medical interest going on inside my body. It seems rather an inferior machine after the high tech of the Harris Birthright Centre. I watch Dr Stott. He is, I decide, well-meaning, cautious and takes life seriously. He is anxious to get it right.

He switches off the machine and turns to us.

'Well, I'm sure you realise, Mrs Merton, your baby is in a serious condition. In my opinion, I feel that induction of labour is unlikely to be successful, that the baby is unlikely to survive it, so I recommend you have a Caesarean today.' Actually, he says a lot more than this, repeating himself, trying to make everything all right, but this is what it boils down to. He turns to a male underling. 'Do you know if the theatres are free at the moment?'

'No, one's booked till three and the other has a section at the moment.'

Hang on a moment, I think.

'I don't want to have a Caesarean,' I say.

---

* *Not his real name*

Dr Stott looks momentarily a bit put out.

'Well, it's up to you, obviously, but the alternative is to let Nature take its course. But you might not go into labour for weeks. And the baby might die inside you and then you'll have to have a Caesarean anyway. So I think a Caesarean now is the best course of action.'

'Do you think she has a chance of surviving?' I ask.

'Well, it's very difficult to tell,' replies Dr Stott, shifting about uncomfortably. 'She's not moving, and it doesn't look like a diaphragmatic hernia any more. She might survive and be severely handicapped. We can't really tell till she's out. Anyway, I'll leave you to think about it for a while,' and he leaves, followed by the underlings, who are glad to have seen such an Interesting Case.

Nicky and Nick and I look at each other.

'I don't understand this,' I say. 'I came here early in the morning to get induced, and now I'm being advised to have a Caesarean. I couldn't really follow the reasoning behind what he said. What did he mean, 'let Nature take its course?' If she is going to die anyway, as he seems to think, why give me a Caesarean?'

'I know,' says Nicky with a sigh. 'Remember, doctors in hospitals almost assume you'll have a Caesarean if the baby's breech. Or at least a managed second stage, with forceps and everything. They don't think it's possible to give birth naturally to a breech baby.'

'And the other thing is did he really think she was going to die? He said she might be handicapped.'

When Nicky replies, I find it difficult to concentrate on what she says. It is as if my brain is paralysed. My mind, normally so quick, seems stuck. I am having to force ideas into shape using words, and then repeating them slowly till they sink in. It is like running a film through in slow motion.

While we are still talking about it, the door opens sharply and a tall young doctor with dark hair walks in.

'Mrs Merton, I'm James Bernard*; I'm the registrar in charge

---

* *Not his real name*

today. So, what have you decided?' he asks. He seems self-assured to the point of insensitivity.

'We haven't yet. But I'll probably want to be induced, as planned.'

'Well, I'm happy to have you induced if that's what you want,' Dr Bernard replies, in a tone of voice that implies the opposite, 'but I'm telling you, if you're not having strong contractions an hour after your waters have been broken, then I'll put you on syntocinon without any question. Not because of the baby,' he adds. 'It's purely selfish. I don't want to be working here late.' No one says anything. We just look at him. He examines me rather roughly and says to Nicky, 'She's 2cm dilated. Bulging membranes and presenting part tangible. So you can proceed with the ARM' (artificial rupture of the membranes) 'as soon as she's been X-rayed.'

We heave a sigh of relief when he leaves.

'What a pig,' I remark. 'So that's what a lot of women are up against in hospital.'

'I'm afraid so,' says Nicky.

The next moment, Ruth puts her head around the door.

'Hello, I just came to see how things were. Have you had your waters broken yet?'

Nicky explains what is happening. 'If Dr Bernard had his way, she'd be having a section or being stuffed with syntocinon by now.'

'I know,' says Ruth, and shakes her head. 'But what do you want, Chrissy?'

'Well, I want to be induced, but I'd like more information before I go ahead with it. I want to know what Alice's chances of survival are exactly. Or if nobody knows, I want to know that. So I want to talk to the paediatric consultant.'

'Dr Gamsu? Well he's meeting at this moment with Kypros and Dr Stott to discuss your case. Look, I'll ask one of them to come and talk to you as soon as they're free. Now, you need to go down and be X-rayed anyway. Take this form with you.'

After talking to Ruth I feel quite different from how I felt after talking to Dr Bernard. No wonder women often feel their experience of birth in hospital is out of their hands, and are left with fear and dissatisfaction.

On the way down to the X-ray Department, I ask Nicky whether it isn't dangerous to X-ray Alice.

'That's the least of her problems,' Nicky comments wryly. 'And unfortunately they always do this in hospital if they know the baby's breech. They want to make sure there's enough room in your pelvis.'

It seems so unlikely that Nature would design a fully-grown woman the wrong size to be able to give birth to a breech baby at 37 weeks, I think. If she'd been breech but healthy would they still X-ray her, knowing the danger of causing cancer? What I didn't know yet is the danger of X-raying a women's ovaries. And this is the second time they have been X-rayed. When I was seven I had two X-rays on my lower back.

We sit on hard wooden pews among people in dressing gowns in wheelchairs and children sitting on their mother's laps. I am the only pregnant woman. I remember Sara telling me about a midwife who went to Dubai to learn about traditional midwifery. She could turn a baby round inside the mother; she could tell by looking at you if there was enough room for the baby. What I don't know at this point is that cranial osteopaths also can usually turn a baby round. But conventional medicine relies so much on machines now.

I am asked to stand very still between a frame, front on and sideways. We wait a while for the X-rays to be processed, then one has to be done again. It is about an hour and a half before we are back up in the labour room. It is now eleven-thirty.

'You really appreciate this room after visiting the rest of the hospital,' Nick remarks.

'Yes,' I agree. 'All it needs now is a little drinks cabinet fridge in the corner.'

'Well, at least we've got a TV.' Nick points to the scanner monitor. 'Pity there's no remote control.'

'Hey, I'm feeling quite faint with hunger. Can you pass me the bag, darling?'

We are all nibbling prunes, crisps and nuts when we are interrupted by the entry of Dr Bernard. He looks at me eating, but says nothing. I know he is thinking about Caesareans and anaesthetics. He looks at the X-rays instead.

'Yes, they look fine. So you're ready to be induced now, aren't you?'

'Well, I'm just waiting to see Dr Gamsu before that. We're expecting him very soon,' I reply.

'Oh. OK,' he says, briefly, and leaves. Nicky and I grin at each other.

'Well, he didn't like the delay or my eating, did he?' I remark.

'It can't do any harm now. The food's got plenty of time to leave your stomach, still,' Nicky says.

'I wonder how many women are given Caesareans because they're weak from not being allowed to eat anything in case they need a Caesarean,' I muse. 'Anyway, I'm going to rest while we wait.'

I lie down on my side on the narrow bed and Nick lies beside me, back to back. We have just about enough room.

'You do look sweet, you two,' says Nicky, looking up from writing in the Midwifery Notes book.

I lie there breathing gently, relaxing and just focusing on the question of what to do, comforted by the feel of Nick's warm back against mine.

Alice may live and be severely physically and mentally handicapped, she may die before or after she is born, or she may even live and be OK. Extremely unlikely, but you have to include the possibility of miracles when dealing with an unknown outcome. Could I stand having a severely handicapped child who may live for years? How would Nick take it? But what say have I in it anyway? What difference would it make if I decide I don't want a handicapped child? These thoughts have been tossing around in my head and in our conversation on and off for the last few hours, and each time I feel as if my brain is half anaesthetised, and as soon as one thought is clearly present in my head, the previous one seems to have disappeared. But lying here, relaxing, is different. I don't try to sort it out. After all, reasoning and logic are getting us nowhere. I just hold the situation, wordlessly, in my mind. I suppose I am using the right, creative, non-verbal side of my brain rather than the usual left, analytical side. And soon a sense of peace and clarity comes over me. I know that all there is to do is trust everything will work out: to do everything there is to have her live, and then she either will or won't. I will have to accept the risk of her being handicapped, and trust that everything will happen for the best.

From that moment on, my experience takes on a different quality. I seem to have fewer thoughts, I feel very present to whatever is going on, and, despite the extreme uncertainty about the immediate future, I feel much freer. From now on, every action is guided by my commitment to have Alice live, without any attachment to the outcome. I tell Nick of my decision. He completely understands and agrees.

Eventually Doctor Gamsu comes to see us. He is a large, gentle man with a long grey beard, and very polite manners. I am touched at his obvious concern for my situation. I ask him what he thinks Alice's chances of survival are.

'Well, Mrs Merton, I'm afraid we really don't know. It's pretty clearly not a diaphragmatic hernia now; Dr Nicolaides thinks it could be Arthrogryposis, which is a weak-muscle condition, but I feel it would have become evident before this late stage. The symptoms would have been there much earlier. So I'm sorry I can't be more helpful.'

'What are the chances of a baby surviving when she hasn't moved for a week or two?'

'Well,' he says, almost apologetically, 'very slim, I'm afraid, though there are the few exceptions. One does hear of the occasional miracle.'

'So do you consider the chance to be 1% or 10% or what?'

'Well, I really wouldn't like to put a figure on it. We really don't know. I'm very sorry...'

'That's OK,' I say. 'This is useful. At least I'm completely clear where we are now: that we don't know. And Nick and I have become completely clear that my course of action is simply to do everything to have the baby live if she can.'

'Well, I admire your resolve, Mrs Merton,' he says, and stands up.

'And thank you very much for coming to see us,' I say, smiling.

He gives a little half-bow, inclines his head and gently leaves the room.

It is now two-thirty, and we are going ahead with the ARM. As Nicky attaches the two black belts around my enormous tummy and sets up the CTG machine, Nick takes the first photo of me, looking like a hippopotamus.

'This is like the start of an expedition,' I remark, and give a royal wave to the camera.

The graph starts to trace out a straight line.

I watch, and wait, unalarmed, as Nicky fetches a hospital midwife, who has a look, and says, 'I think this machine isn't working very well. I'd proceed with the ARM anyway, if I were you.' I notice I have no thoughts or feelings. I am just here. I know Alice is alive still. Nicky puts a gloved hand inside me to feel my cervix, and is surprised at what she finds.

'You know, I thought James Bernard was exaggerating. You're only 1cm dilated, and her bottom is very high, I can't even feel it. He said her presenting part was tangible. I'm afraid I dare not rupture the membranes without checking there's an operating theatre free. With all this fluid you might get a prolapsed cord.'

This means that the middle of the cord might come out with the fluid, because of the gap between Alice's bottom and my cervix, and that would risk her oxygen supply being cut off. Nicky calls the midwife (Kate) and tells her. 'Do you think you could find Dr Bernard and tell him I can't proceed unless there's a theatre free.'

She undoes the black belts and we settle in for another wait.

'Well, what shall we talk about now?' says Nick, brightly.

'We could have guesses as to who's going to come through that door next,' I suggest. 'This is an Alan Aykbourne play, isn't it? We haven't seen Angela yet today, have we?'

'No. Anyway, I'm going to put some music on. What would you like?'

'The Flame.'

'Just for a change?'

Kate comes in and says both the theatres are in use at the moment, and Dr Bernard is in one of them, so she can't talk to him yet. 'OK, I'll take this chance to go and call Katrina,' Nicky says. As soon as she has left, who should come in but Angela.

'Hello, darling, how are you? You've had a tough time this morning, haven't you? Sorry I couldn't get down any earlier. It's been really hectic up there.'

'Don't worry. I know how busy you all are. Did you have loads of calls after the Natalie Robertson article?'

'Yes; it's always like that when he's been in the papers. But it's a bit toned down by the surrogate mother story.'

'What's that?' we ask.

'Oh, don't you know? She's coming here tomorrow to be induced. She's carrying the baby of a woman who has a rare blood condition which means she can't get pregnant, but one of her eggs was used, and her husband's sperm, and the embryo was planted inside this young woman. She's only twenty. I couldn't do it, you know, even if I was paid £3,000.'

'£3,000? Is that what she got? That seems a lot, but I suppose not if you think about what she had to go through, and all the possible risks. I wonder what she'll feel like after the baby's born.'

'Yes, it must be odd, knowing that it's not your baby. Anyway, darling, I must dash, I'm afraid. I'm so glad you're all right. We're all thinking of you upstairs, you know.'

At four o'clock, Nicky comes back and says, 'Well, here's a new development. There's a message from Dr Gamsu saying that if your membranes haven't been ruptured, then we should stop. Apparently the staffing levels in the neonatal unit aren't good enough this weekend to handle this kind of situation so we'll have to wait till Monday. He's coming down soon to explain to you in person. They've really mucked you about, I'm afraid. I'm sorry about this.'

'No, it's fine, honestly,' I say. 'It's been a useful day. I've got much clearer now, and at least I've got the X-ray out of the way.'

'It's not a bad hotel, this,' Nick adds. 'Good food, plenty of action. Not much on TV, though. Just some black-and-white films about babies deep-sea diving.'

Nicky laughs. 'You two are so positive. I don't know how you do it.'

Nick and I smile at each other.

At four-thirty, Dr Gamsu explains the situation to us, as promised, in person.

'You see, Mrs Merton, I'm very sorry to have stopped the induction, but there's no senior registrar on this weekend, just a locum and two house doctors. I do apologise for all this delay.'

He seems so upset for me that I find myself reassuring him that it is fine, and thanking him for his concern for my baby, in making sure there are good doctors there for her. I really am touched. Maybe my calm decision about Alice affected him and made him look to see if he could increase her chances in any way. It is going to be a bit of a strain having to wait through another two days, though, especially as my tummy is so large and tight. It is nearly two days since I came to the hospital to be drained but went home without it having been done. I have a suspicion that my labour will start soon anyway.

It is five o'clock when we pack up our 'hotel room' and go upstairs to the Harris Birthright Centre. There are no patients and we are aware of an atmosphere of decided frivolity as we walk along the corridor. Kypros, Douglas, Angela and Ruth are joking together and teasing each other. Kypros turns to us.

'What are you doing here?' he asks. 'You should have gone home ages ago. Go on, go home!'

'We came to give you a present,' I say, smiling.

He sits down on the floor in front of me with his back to me.

'Massage my shoulders,' he growls, pretending to be stern, and the others laugh. I give him the box of Nick's cards that we have brought with us.

'What's this? Hey, did you paint these, Nick?' he asks, looking through them, and Angela passes them around to admiring murmurs. 'Are the originals for sale?'

'Well, I've sold all these, I'm afraid, but I've got plenty more.'

'I like them. They're really nice. I'd like to see more.'

Then he stands up, grabs my hand and marches quickly into the scan room, the others following. As soon as we are in there, he suddenly looks very grave.

'I'm so sorry this disastrous mess has happened to you, all this changing of plans…'

'It's fine, Kypros, we don't mind,' I assure him.

'Well, it shouldn't have happened. You've been badly treated.' He stops and shakes his head, then turns to the scanner.

'Now let's have a look at this baby,' he says, and is soon examining the screen. I can see that the fluid has filled up around her lungs again just 24 hours after it was drained off.

'Now, to give the baby the best possible chance, I'll drain the pleural oedema again on Monday around nine o'clock, just before the ARM. But if you need anything over the weekend, just call me anytime at home. Ruth, can you give her my home number?'

Ruth scribbles it on a scrap of paper as Kypros helps me off the scan table.

'Now get out of here,' he says, 'get off home!'

Chapter Seven

Birth

What is required is courage. And courage is one of the easier ones. It's not like you go into a situation where you are essentially weak of heart and afraid and somehow by a great effort of will you screw up your courage to overcome your cowardice to do this thing, even though it is scaring the pants off you while you are doing it – that ain't how it works. Courage comes from 'heart' – 'coeur' in French, 'corazon' in Spanish – and courage means you see the importance of this thing in front of you so strong and so seriously and you have so much heart and you care about it so much that you are single-mindedly intent on doing it, and you don't even consider whether you are afraid or not. You love somebody enough, or you love everybody enough, that it is worth your while to do it.

Mind at Play
Stephen Gaskin

In high mountains, there is small room for mistake.
The Snow Leopard
Peter Matthiessen

We haven't been in bed long when I realise that I am going into labour. The pain across my lower back is quite strong, and I am getting mild contractions. It isn't surprising really. I guessed this would happen. Oh, God, I think, just when I want a good night's sleep; but there is nothing for it. This is it. At least it is working without syntocinon. That is something, I think gleefully.

At half past eleven I phone Nicky. She says that as I can talk through the contractions, they are still very mild, so we should leave it a couple more hours. But as we are talking I feel a warm liquid trickling out on to the bedclothes. My waters have broken. They seem to be leaking out slowly, so there doesn't seem to be any danger of a prolapsed cord. But Nicky decides not to take any chances, so she and Katrina drive straight over. They wrap me in a blanket and carry me down to the car, making a seat out of their hands, the way you are taught in Girl Guides. Nick and I get in the back with the bag of clothes and food, and we drive back to King's again.

We are given a huge room this time. It still has the pretty curtains and rag-rolled walls, but it is more like a dance studio than a hotel room. A rather hot dance studio. There is a bed, with the statutory white sheets and white cellular blanket, an armchair, a resuscitaire (rather like a simplified incubator) and a vast expanse of hard, dark linoleum floor. It doesn't feel homely.

'Well, there's going to be quite a performance later on,' I remark. 'I guess we'll need all this space.'

As I get on to the bed, the water starts to come out in earnest. Maybe Alice's bottom has been acting as a stopper and now she has moved. Nicky and Katrina mop it all up as it pours out (there must have been at least two litres) and change the sheet. My tummy is noticeably less taut now.

Nicky fetches me some entonox, and then a young doctor comes in to examine me. She has all the brusque authority of someone quite junior, and I feel rather wary of her. When I see her get out a speculum, one of those horrible phallic metal things, I guess what she is about to do, and started to breathe in entonox. She thinks I am taking it for the contractions, and starts to tell me not to use it, as my contractions are going to get much worse later on. She obviously thinks I am some kind of inexperienced wimp, and has probably never seen entonox used for the pains caused by medical intervention. I feel rather affronted, and take off the mask to try to explain to her. At this point, however, she has the speculum inside me, and with a classic doctor's understatement, 'This is going to be a little uncomfortable', she pinches what feels like a large chunk out of my cervix. I am angry and hurt. I could have prevented that pain if I'd been breathing entonox. She also didn't ask my permission to take a cervical smear. But I feel like crying, so I say nothing and try to forget about it.

My cervix (what is left of it) hasn't dilated any more, so at three o'clock Nicky and Katrina decide to go home and get a couple of hours' sleep. Nicky finds a dimmer switch for the lights, then fetches a couple of large black birthing cushions for Nick to sleep on. We settle down for the night and try to get whatever sleep we can. I just lie there for a while, feeling the contractions increasing in strength and becoming distinctly uncomfortable.

I am still upset by the young doctor's actions. It is the first time I have felt that I wasn't properly in communication with someone in the hospital, and am left with something niggling at me. I think of all the stories I have read or heard about women in hospital feeling ignored or not heard, and realise this must be a very common experience for some people. I suspect women are often left for hours in labour, as my mother was, with no comfort; it was probably worse in the days before the father's presence was de rigueur.

Looking down from my high bed, I can see Nick asleep on the birthing cushions on the floor next to me. He is covered in our furry brown rug, that I have known all my life; the car rug that my father used as a little boy. It is comforting to have such a familiar object in such a hard, alien, surrounding. My pictures of a home birth come to mind, with rugs, cushions and soft furnishings. Maybe even a birthing pool, and candlelight. Well, at least I have Nick and my furry rug.

The contractions start getting stronger and more painful. I time the intervals. Five minutes. It is only four-fifteen, but I feel we'd better phone Nicky, so Nick goes off to call her. Once she arrives, things develop into quite a pattern. Every five minutes, just as I am drifting off to sleep, I feel another contraction coming on and take deep breaths of entonox, moaning loudly into the mask as they sweep through me. Nicky, half-asleep in the armchair, says, 'Well done, Chrissy, that's right. Good.' It is amusing in a bizarre kind of way, though I really like her saying it. The contractions are getting increasingly painful. I didn't realise they would be this painful. But at least there is nothing in between. Just resting. So it isn't as bad as a miscarriage, which hurts non-stop for several hours, with no respite.

After hours and hours of this strange half-sleep, I realise I have to pee. Nick helps me down the long corridor to the loo. We stop as another a contraction arrives. It is seven o'clock and the world is beginning to wake up. On the way back I see a young woman walking back into another room with a midwife in uniform.

'That was that surrogate mother,' Nick tells me when we've passed.

'How do you know?' I ask.

'I heard the hospital midwives talking about her on the way to the loo, while you were having a contraction, so I knew she was in that room.'

Nicky tells me that Kypros has been contacted and will be here in an hour to drain Alice's lungs. She turns up the lights in our room and fastens a black CTG belt round my tummy. Then the junior doctor comes back to examine me again. I've got to say something, I think, or this upset will stay with me.

'You know when you examined me earlier,' I tell her, 'I wasn't taking the entonox for contractions, it was for the pain of the examination. I've been using it for weeks in the Harris Birthright Centre.'

'Oh, I see,' she says. I'm not sure if she does, but it doesn't matter. I feel fine now I've said it, and forget about it. She finds I am 6cm dilated, which is 60% of the way, so I am glad it is progressing at a reasonable rate. Anything to avoid the labour-inducing drugs. She also talks about putting a 'Copeland clip' on Alice's behind. This is a little pin which is clipped on to the 'presenting part' of the baby, usually the head, as most babies are born head down, and a lead is connected to the machine which monitors the foetal heartbeat. I think it's a horrible invention, because it probably hurts the baby, and it also means that the mother's movements are restricted. Luckily, Alice's 'presenting part' is her bottom, which is swollen with oedema (water under her skin) so she decides against it, and I just have my abdomen monitored at regular intervals instead.

The contractions become quite frequent, long and extremely painful. Now I am feeling quite desperate. And where is Kypros? Shouldn't he be here by now? It is nearly nine o'clock and I am 8cm dilated. I wonder if the entonox is making much difference, but it is easier to make noises into the mask than out loud. This labour seems to have been going on forever. It is a bad idea, I decide, having this baby. Can't I just go home and sleep and let someone else go through this?

When Kypros finally comes in, I am kneeling on one of the black cushions, wearing only a long T-shirt, with Nicky beside me, encouraging me through every contraction. I have no contact lenses in, and can't really see the woman who follows Kypros in. I look up and find myself saying, 'Kypros, you bastard, where have you been? You're an hour late!'

Kypros looks around in mock astonishment. 'What's going on here?' he asks.

'It's all right, Kypros,' says Nicky patiently, 'she's in transition stage. It's normal.'

'Oh, I don't want to be around anything normal,' he says, and pretends to go. It is a relief to hear his usual jokes. He introduces the woman with him, a colleague of his. She bends down to say Hello and that she is sorry we couldn't have met in better circumstances.

'Don't worry, I'm between contractions,' I say. It is a bit like being drunk. I am squeezing in any bit of fun I can; there is nothing to lose now.

Another contraction overwhelms me, so I'm not aware of Nicky's conversation with Kypros, but she explains to me that he has already been upstairs to start preparing the needles. Suddenly, it seems like the last straw.

'No, I can't, I can't,' I gasp.

'You can,' she says calmly. 'You have to.'

'I want an epidural,' I say suddenly. 'I've had enough pain; I can't take any more.'

'It's too late for an epidural,' she says. 'Women always ask for an epidural in transition; it's normal.'

I rummage around in my mind for anything else that is worrying me. 'What if the needle breaks off inside me? I'm having contractions so often.'

'Don't worry, he can do it between contractions. How long does it take you to do each draining?' she asks him.

'I can do each one in 15 seconds.'

'Oh, all right then,' I reply. 'Let's go.'

Immediately, it's Action Stations. It is like suddenly being part of a *Carry On* film. I am bundled into a wheelchair, still wearing only a Virgin Islands T-shirt, with a sanitary pad stuffed between my legs. I grab the entonox mask as the double doors are held back.

'Here, Nick, you drive this,' says Kypros, indicating the wheelchair. Pulling the entonox cylinder trolley, he marches briskly out into the corridor and starts running. We are weaving all over the place. Hospital wheelchairs are obviously closely related to supermarket trolleys.

'Well, you may be a famous artist but you're a hopeless driver,' Kypros remarks as we race along the deserted corridor and into the lift. A whole retinue of people in 'greens', looking as if they are from an operating theatre, chase after us, and cram into the lift too. I work out later they are obstetricians and paediatricians, frightened I might give birth in the Harris Birthright Centre. I am high on adrenalin and entonox, and when Kypros pushes my abdomen, presumably to feel how tight it is, I tell him brightly,

'There's a baby in there!'

'They do say some stupid things, these women,' he remarks to someone above my head. I don't mind that no one else seems to think it is funny. I feel light-headed and giggly.

'*Carry On Kypros*,' I think to myself, 'starring Chrissy Merton...'

I decide not to say it out loud. Now we are out of the lift and I watch the empty Harris Birthright corridor zip by out of focus as I am pulled along backwards. I see in vague amusement the people in green trotting along beside me, and then I yell full out into the mask as another contraction hits me. 'I've always wanted to do that,' I say and have a fleeting memory of Lisa Minelli screaming under the railway bridge in *Cabaret*, before I am lifted on to the scanning table and have to lie on my back.

I have known for a long time that lying on your back is the worst position to give birth in, because it goes against gravity, but I didn't realise how much more painful the contractions are. As the first one sweeps over me, I know that I have to find a way through. So I just let myself experience the pain totally till it ends each time. That's the only way I can describe it; it's what I am telling myself to do. As I curl my legs up in an involuntary reaction, I hear Nicky's voice saying, 'It's all right, Chrissy, Kypros won't put the needle in while you're having a contraction.'

When the contraction is over I notice that everyone is quiet, not saying a word, though the room is full of people. Suddenly I hear Nick say loudly and cheerfully,

'I say, I say, I say, what's the secret of good delivery?'

'Timing,' I say, removing the mask for a second. Kypros turns round slowly from the scan screen to look in amazement.

'Did you rehearse that?' he asks.

'No, it's a little joke we have,' says Nick casually. If I weren't in such pain I'd giggle. I think it has made all the difference. Somehow I get through each contraction. And between times I become very vociferous. There seems to be a long wait, so I call out, 'Come on, what are we waiting for? There's a baby waiting to be delivered in here.'

'We're just sterilising the needles,' says Kypros. 'We thought it would be better to use sterilised needles on you, Chrissy.'

'Oh, all right,' I say, and go on breathing entonox continuously. I notice that Nicky is talking quietly to the hospital midwife beside me. 'It's run out. Can you get a new one?' Pause. 'How do you get it off?'

I am vaguely aware that they must be changing the entonox cylinders but I don't mind. I am trusting everything. I have to, to go through this. There is no other way. Nick tells me later that he trusted Kypros but was nervous when he realised that the entonox had run out. He was worried I'd really feel the pain. I guess an army of endorphins was racing around my body.

'Now, you'll feel some pressure,' says Kypros as usual, and I feel a slight pain as the needle goes in. Soon I am aware of another contraction coming; I have a few seconds warning.

'Here comes another one,' I say calmly.

'It's all right, the needle's out,' I hear him say as I disappear into it. Even behind all the pain and worry I still appreciate the beauty of the dance we are in, the precision of the timing. I know that it will work out.

Now for the other side. The next contraction has just finished when I feel another needle going in. A few long seconds, willing the contractions to wait, and I feel it come out. It is done! I am gently hauled off the scanning table and bundled back into the wheelchair, elated despite everything, by the courage and resilience I have had to bring to the situation.

'That's the worst of it over now,' says Katrina. 'You won't have to go through anything like that again.'

That's known as prophetic irony in novels.

Back in the labour room, squatting on the floor, Nicky explains to me that the next bit is like Hard Work. 'Now you don't mind Hard Work, do you?' I shake my head. She and Katrina get the birthing stool out for me, made of curved wood, about the height of a milking stool, cover it in a white sheet, and I sit on it, with Nick sitting on another little stool behind me. Between contractions I lean against him, and then squat on the floor like a frog for each contraction.

'Now is the time to push,' explains Nicky, 'so use that urge to push, hold your breath and push as hard as you can.'

It is impossible using the entonox as it numbs me slightly. I can just ride the contraction without pushing, so I put it aside. But I thought you had a strong urge to push in the second stage. These contractions don't feel any different really. But I can't be bothered to say so. Between each contraction I just appreciate the complete peace of feeling my body relaxing and resting, and then I have to exert myself for the next one, and make my body squat and push.

Nicky is encouraging me, as she kneels down, her head near the floor, watching. This seems to go on and on, squatting and pushing, sitting back and relaxing. Katrina offers Nick some tea. 'Can I have some?' I ask.

'No, you're not allowed any yet. You can have some water.'

I know it is in case I have to have a Caesarean, but I feel momentarily left out, like a child when the adults can have some chocolate and you can't till you've tidied your bedroom. But I am getting too tired to feel much. I exist in this strange world of contraction, pause, contraction, pause, contraction, pause.

After a while Katrina suggests that we set up the end of the bed in the way it was designed, as a birthing stool. I watch, mildly interested, as the end of the bed is removed, so that just the metal sides are sticking out, and two platforms for my feet are pulled forward. This is all being set up by a kind young man who describes himself as 'the technician'. I learn later he is a house doctor. He sets up two drips of glucose and syntocinon, the former to give me energy, the latter to speed up the contractions. The needle going sideways into my arm is painful. I never realised before, when I saw pictures of people with drips, how much it hurts. It is some time before I can forget about it. I am put on the end of the bed, with Nick behind me. Then the hospital midwife comes up to me with two black foetal monitoring belts. She puts one round my abdomen, quite high up, and then I ask, 'Is the other one for Nick?'

She thinks this is really funny, and keeps chuckling to herself and saying, 'For Nick. That's funny!' as she fastens it around my abdomen lower down.

Then a new routine starts. For each contraction I put my arms around Katrina's neck, as she stands firm and holds me under my arms. That way she can take much of my weight and I can concentrate on pushing. I am trying to get the hang of this idea of completely holding my breath, and she is coaching me and encouraging me. 'Well done, Chrissy, that's right, now push once more. That's it!'

Each time I feel a contraction coming I know I have to move, put my arms around Katrina and push, and each time I feel it is more than I can manage. It is the last thing in the world I want to do; I just want to lie there. And each time I somehow simply do it. I feel I want to cry, but even crying is far too much effort. And between times I begin to really value the rest, the space of not contracting. I shut my eyes and feel my body, simply being at peace. And each time that the thought creeps into my mind that it won't last, that I'll have to move and push again, I pull myself back to experiencing how beautiful it is to lean back against Nick and relax.

Soon a young woman comes into the room and speaks to Nicky. She is good-looking, with short hair and a calm, open air about her, and green overalls on. I realise that I saw her in the corridor with us when we were racing to the Harris Birthright Centre. Nicky introduces her as Sarah Creighton, the obstetrician who is going to deliver Alice. Sarah explains to me in a soft, clear manner that I'm not moving as fast as they would like, so she's going to give me 20 minutes more and then, if Alice isn't out, I'll have a Caesarean. She leaves the room, and I hear myself say, 'Just let me go to sleep. Just let me go to sleep.'

'You've only got 20 more minutes, Chrissy,' says Katrina. 'Just give it everything for twenty minutes, then you can sleep.' It is the perfect thing to say, to give me an end, somewhere in sight. The next contraction starts and I move forward and hang, holding my breath for the first push. And then something unexpected happens. As well as Katrina's encouragements, I can hear Nick now, saying, 'Come on, darling, you can do it! Push!' I know I have to get this baby out, now. It just tips the scales, and somewhere I find yet another last untapped reserve of determination. I make myself hold my breath and be completely silent for a few seconds, letting all the energy go into the push, and none into any sound from my mouth.

'That's brilliant, Chrissy, she's coming down,' says Nicky. 'She really moved that time,' she tells me as I lie back. I can't even manage a smile. I use the next few minutes to recharge my batteries for the next time, then up again, and once again I give it everything. A few more contractions then I really feel something.

'Ow, it's burning, it's burning,' I say, unable to sit back, as I feel my skin stretched open and taut.

'That's good, that's fine, that's just her bottom coming out,' says Nicky. 'Just hang on for the next contraction.' The burning eases a bit and I see a flash of light through my closed eyelids, and open my eyes to see Nicky with her camera and Sarah turning around to motion to her to stop.

'It's all right,' says Katrina, beside her, below me, both of them waiting for Alice to come out. 'They've asked us to take photos.'

The next contraction, and I feel a slippery little body slide out of me. Only her head is still inside. Sarah suggests I try to push, but it doesn't work, and I wait for the next contraction, when, giving a wide-open yell, I feel her head move through that impossible gap. I look down to see her, lying in Sarah's arms, relief that the labour is over flooding through me.

She is completely still, her skin a grey-blue tinge, and her little bottom bruised purple. She has dark hair, matted with blood, but

I can't see her face yet.

'We're just going to cut the cord and take her over to the resuscitaire,' Sarah says, so I lie back and keep saying, 'I did it. I did it.' It still hasn't sunk in that I've actually got her out. I've been living with the impossibility of it, and the imminent Caesarean for what seems like an eternity, and it is slowly sinking in that she really is out. There will be no Caesarean now. No more pushing. It is over. She is out. Then I realise that Katrina is talking to me, explaining that she is going to give me a shot of syntometrine in my thigh, to expel the placenta, so I say, 'Just give me a chance to get some entonox.' I pick up the mask, relieved that I don't have to feel the pain of anything any more. I feel a strange slippery thing slither out of me, and glance down at what seems to me a huge placenta, liver-coloured, with interesting coloured lights in it. The young 'technician' removes the drip needle from my arm, and then I lie back, shut my eyes and concentrate all my attention on Alice, on the little spirit I have grown so close to over the last few weeks. 'It's all right,' I tell her in my head, 'you can do it. You can come through. I'm here. You can do it.'

I can vaguely hear Katrina saying to Sarah, 'I wouldn't stitch it. We always leave small tears like that, and they heal just fine.' I really can count on those two a hundred per cent.

I ask to see Alice.

There are three paediatricians around the resuscitaire. One is holding a little hand pump that is pumping oxygen into Alice's mouth, and two others are attaching drips to her. The light is on over her little bed, keeping her warm, but I can't see her face. Nicky helps me into the wheelchair and moves me over. Nick stands beside me and we look at our little baby, lying in an incubator.

Her face is puffy, swollen with oedema, and her eyes are closed. Her knees seem to be drawn up, and over to one side. She has a white cloth over her body to keep her warm. She is completely still, and hardly looks alive. She is my baby, and I love her.

I start to talk to her gently, so she can hear my voice, just saying,

'Alice, I'm here, you'll be all right.' Part of me feels a bit stupid. Everyone else is so silent, concentrating on what they are doing. But I know that if I don't talk to her, I might regret it. Maybe she hears and is helped, maybe she doesn't. But I am going to do everything.

As the paediatricians move her on to a kind of moveable resuscitaire, the doors are pushed open and Kypros rushes in. He goes straight over to Alice and looks carefully at her. 'Now is that talipes?' he says to himself, looking at her feet. He stands looking worried and thoughtful as they wheel her out and Nick turns to help Katrina remake the bed. Suddenly I want to comfort Kypros, to let him know it is all OK, whatever happens. He starts to talk to me without looking at me properly. 'She's obviously not at all well, but they've taken her off to the Intensive Care Unit and...'

I open my mouth to say something and to my surprise feel one of my bottom front teeth catch on an upper one, and a little piece chip off.

'Ow!' I say, putting my hand to my mouth.

'What happened?' he asks.

'I just chipped my tooth,' I tell him.

'Well, it's not one of the usual complications of pregnancy, but with you, Chrissy, anything's possible!' He's brightened up again.

'And Kypros, I feel very peaceful..'

'It's all that entonox...'

'No, I mean, whatever happens happens. We've done everything. So I'm at peace...'

He looks at me for a moment then reaches out his hand and touches my cheek. 'You're great,' he says, and goes.

'Do you want to lie down again now?' asks Nicky. I look around and see they have remade the bed with a smooth clean sheet and plumped up the pillows.

'Yes, OK.' My body feels strange. As I lie down I feel so exhausted it seems as if I'll never recover. It is way beyond anything I've ever experienced. Katrina starts to say something about how brilliant it was that I'd done it, I'd given birth squatting, and I say, 'I'm sure I'm going to appreciate it, but at the moment I don't want to remember it.'

I can't bear to think of what has just happened, it is too painful. My body has been through hell, and I don't want to remember it at all. Even speaking is quite an effort. Just being in my body is exhausting. And there is this strange gap.

'Are you all right, darling?' I ask Nick, feeling the comfort of holding his hand.

'I'm fine,' he says, stroking my hair. 'I feel almost guilty for not being a woman.'

'Would you like some Aqua Libra and ginger cake?' asks Nicky.

'Yes, please,' I reply. I don't know if I do. I don't seem to know anything. And there is something strange about this room. What is it? I start to sip the Aqua Libra and nibble the cake, and hold Nick's hand. I am trying to work it out. There is the same big arc lamp hung from the ceiling. The hospital midwife is mopping the floor and cleaning up, and Katrina is examining my placenta in the little room next door. I seem to have been in this room forever, and it is like being in a nightmare, like the dreams I used to have as a child when I had a temperature. When I speak, or when anyone else speaks, I feel as if I am constantly coming back from a second's amnesia. That's what it's like. I tell Nicky.

'It's exhaustion,' she explains. 'Normally a woman has something to counteract it, because she has her baby, but you haven't got her here, so you're really feeling it.'

Yes, I've got no baby. I've had this little being living with me, inside me, part of me, for months, and suddenly, she isn't here. There is just silence in my body where there had been life.

I start to cry, sobbing into the bed, and Nick puts his arms around me. 'I'm sick of being strong,' I say. 'I just want to be normal. I just want to have a normal baby.' I cry and cry, which is a bit of a relief, though even crying is exhausting. And that unreal feeling persists, as if I'm not quite here all the time.

After a while a nurse comes in and speaks to Nicky.

'Right, shall we go down and see Alice? They're ready to have us now.'

The mere thought of sitting up is horrible.

'Give me a bit longer,' I say. I can't move; I can't. And in my head, I am telling myself for the future, 'Chrissy, remember what it is like now. Remember this exhaustion and forgive yourself. Don't be hard on yourself for not rushing down to be with Alice. Forgive yourself. You are giving everything you can.' They start getting the wheelchair ready.

'Do you want to put some clothes on?' asks Katrina. I let them put on a pair of Nick's underpants over the sanitary pad, and my baggy coloured trousers. I want to stay lying down, but luckily they realise it is important that I go downstairs and are gently helping me. Once again – thank God! – they are following what I am committed to, rather than letting me do what I feel like doing. They know that whatever happens now I will remember forever. They pick me up and put me in the wheelchair. 'Are you OK like that?' asks Nicky. 'Yes, I'm OK.' She pushes me out into the corridor, and we all go down to the Baby Unit on the fourth floor.

We have to wash our hands with special sterilising fluid, and turn off the long-handled taps with our elbows. Then the Sister steps forward and says, 'Parents only, please,' quite abruptly, so we agree to meet Nicky and Katrina outside afterwards, and Nick wheels me in.

Here she is, lying under an infra-red lamp, covered in a kind of light silver sheeting, with a tube up her nose, and a tube in her mouth, a drip attached to one hand, and something taped to her foot. Little monitors and wires are taped to her chest, which is moving as she breathes, though 'breathing' seems a strange word for it. Her face is still very puffy, and she has a knitted bonnet on to keep her head warm. A label above her says 'Alice Merton, 6lbs 1oz'.

I put my hand over the side of the incubator and touch her hand. For the first time, I touch my baby. She closes her fingers around one of my fingers and holds it. I am filled with wonder. Here is this tiny little human being, completely new, as Rosa was, but she is mine, she is our baby. I feel enormous pride at the privilege of being her mother. I have just given more for this baby than I have ever given for anyone. More than I thought it possible to give. I know what it is to be a mother: the total, unconditional, undeniable love.

A nurse comes over with a polaroid camera and asks me if I'd like a photo of her. She takes it and leaves us with the developing polaroid. I hold the photo in my lap but don't watch it as the picture gradually appears. This time is precious. Nick is listening to the locum woman doctor telling him about Alice's condition. He is stroking her feet, which she is waving gently, despite her locked hips. But I hardly listen. I am looking at Alice. As she clasps and unclasps her grip on my finger, I stroke her hand and tell her everything there is to say.

'I'm here, darling. It's OK, I'm here. I know you love us, and you know we love you.'

I just keep talking, telling her what beautiful little hands she has, anything so she can hear my voice, the voice she's heard so much when she was inside me. Perhaps she can't hear, perhaps she is too far gone. Perhaps her spirit understands what I am saying, perhaps not. What matters is that I give her all my love, all my attention, while the dials on the wall of machines whir and click, and people watch them, fiddle with them, and adjust things. I don't know how long we have been here, but after a while I start to feel a bit faint, and put my head down. I am given a glass of water, but told, 'You'll have to go if you're feeling faint. We can't have parents fainting in here.' So we leave.

'I'll be back, Alice,' I tell her. 'We're just going upstairs.'

The sense of madness, the amnesia, lifted when I was with Alice, but back in the delivery room it returns again. I feel numbed and hardly present. As we arrive back up, there is a phone call from the fourth floor to say that Alice is in decline again, and we can't visit again till she stabilises.

'I thought we were ushered out rather quickly,' I say. 'Something was just happening as we were leaving.'

'It'll probably be like this for a while,' says Katrina, 'up and down.'

Nicky tells us that she has arranged for Nick and me to have a double room for tonight, so that Nick can look after me. It is so thoughtful of them. After that I will stay on in the maternity ward. Then they go to find us some food, as it is about six o'clock. It isn't very exciting food. Little pizzas, mashed potato and sweet corn. It all seems to be yellow and tepid. But we eat it. Nicky and Katrina go off to find where our room is, so we can move, but they come straight back in.

'They've just called us from Intensive Care. Alice is dying; we must go down now.'

I can see Katrina has tears in her eyes, but I can't feel anything. So this is it. I notice I'm not surprised. We rush down in the lift and through the doors of the Baby Unit, stopping to wash our hands again. This time I insist that Nicky and Katrina come in too.

There is a screen around Alice's incubator. I take one look at her and know she isn't here any more. The young paediatrician, Bobby Gasper, standing beside her incubator, is looking very sad. 'Her heart's slowing down now,' he says. 'She's just kept going by the oxygen.'

I reach in and touch her lifeless little hand.

'She's still warm.' I start to cry, and can hear Katrina crying too. 'Thank you for living four and a half hours, Alice. Thank you.' I know this really is goodbye now, and through all the numbness I can feel the wrench, the pain of losing any last hope.

'Do you want to take out the tubes, or do you want them to?' Nicky asks me.

'They can do it,' I say.

We are shown into a small room with two beds in it. Nick is crying. I hold his hand. Then we sit and wait, are brought cups of tea, and talk about the different nurses and doctors: the kind young paediatrician, Bobby, the nurse who took a photo of Alice, the abrupt sister, who stopped Nicky and Katrina coming in.

Then a nurse brings Alice in, with a little dress on, laid out in a Moses basket, followed by a younger nurse. The older nurse is Scottish, and a bit nervous, I feel. Perhaps she is used to only having the parents there, and doesn't know how to relate to Nicky and Katrina. I try to put her at her ease, thanking her, but that probably makes it worse, because I am smiling, not crying.

She goes through the routine of undressing her, and washing her little body all over, gently getting the blood out of her hair. Then she puts a towel on my lap and hands her to me so I can dry her. I look at the bruise on her hand where the needle had gone in and the big purple bruise on her bottom where she was knocked as I tried for hours to push her out. And, worse, I see the plasters on her chest and back where they inserted needles to try to drain the fluid from around her lungs. I heard Nick being told that much in the Intensive Care Unit. I feel very little. I just dry her, and Nicky takes lots of photos. Then the nurse cuts a little lock of her soft beautiful dark hair and puts it in a screw-top tube for me to keep. She puts a nappy on her and asks if I have any special dress I want her to wear. I haven't, so she takes a brand-new little white dress out of its packet and puts it on her. I think it is wonderful, how much care is being taken, how much thought has gone into this. We take lots more photos, and call Bobby in to take a group photo, with me smiling wanly, like a ghost.

Back in the big, empty dance studio, Nick wraps me in the brown furry rug, then we pack up our things and they wheel me out. I am glad to leave that room, as it seems filled with the nightmare sense of exhaustion.

Outside, the full moon is shining in a clear, cold sky. 'A moon like Alice,' I think to myself as we cross the car park. It can only be early evening, but time seems to have lost all its patterns. We seem to have been in an endless night-time of artificial lights and long corridors. The moon looks refreshing and beautiful.

Then I see the young surrogate mother, with a few other people, family or friends, walking slowly and carefully up the hill, going home without the baby who had lived inside her for nine months, but £3,000 richer. I wonder how she feels. Is she happy to have given the baby to its real parents, or does she feel that same emptiness and loneliness I feel now Alice has gone? Our situations seem so different – even the fact that she can walk seems amazing to me in my weakened state – yet I wonder.

Nicky and Katrina drive us home. I can just about get from the wheelchair into their car, and they nearly carry me up the two flights of stairs into the flat. Cleo is at the door, looking uncomfortable and unsure of what is happening.

We sit around drinking tea, feeling we don't want to break up the group just yet. We have been through so much together. It feels as if we've climbed Everest and are now back at base camp for the last time, ready to fly home. We go over what people said; I discover what was going on outside the doors while I was trying to push Alice out, how Nicky valiantly staved off the male doctors who were trying to make me have a Caesarean.

'The whole ward was rooting for you,' says Katrina. 'Every time one of us came out, the nurses and midwives would say, "How's it going? Where's she got to now?"'

'That was probably the first natural delivery of a breech birth that's ever happened in King's,' says Nicky. 'I bet they didn't know it was possible.'

'Well, I was amazed at how you kept going,' says Nick. 'You've got incredible resilience. And strength. I don't know how you did it.'

'Did you think I'd stop?'

'Yes, I kept thinking you wouldn't move with the next contraction, and you'd end up having a Caesarean.'

'It was amazing when you cheered me on!'

'Well, when they started to put up the stirrups, I could see you were on your last legs and I knew I had to do something. I'm glad it worked.'

I smile at the 'last legs'. I don't think he'd noticed how quite how appropriate that phrase was.

Eventually, around nine o'clock they leave us, and I drop off immediately into a deep sleep. I wake around four in the morning and that terrible exhaustion, the paralysed sense of madness, has gone. In an instant I remember that Alice is dead, that it is all over, and I sob and sob in Nick's arms.

Chapter Eight

Healing

Life is love; enjoy it.
Life is mystery; know it.
Life is a promise; fulfil it.
Life is sorrow; overcome it.
Life is a song; sing it.
Life is a struggle; accept it.
Life is a tragedy; embrace it.
Life is an adventure; dare it.
Source unknown

We wake again at about nine o'clock, into a strange emptiness. The whole future that we have created, that has shaped our life minute by minute, for nearly two months, is over. Here is the past, clear, vivid and unchangeable, filling my mind. Alice is dead. I am no longer pregnant. I am no longer a mother. Or am I? I am a childless mother. And I am worn out, physically and mentally spent. I notice, as I cry in Nick's arms again, that there is also a sense of relief. I am able to sleep deeply without indigestion or backache. There is no more pain to go through, no needles, no labour. My next future to live into is the long job of healing myself.

Nick gets up, and as I lie in bed I start to notice other things. The triumph of giving birth to Alice as I wanted, and of knowing that we did everything we could to save her. I trusted in things working out as they should, and they had. I hadn't had a Caesarean. Alice wasn't going to live on as a vegetable. She hadn't died before birth, and I had been able to hold on to this tiny thread of hope to pull me through the ordeal of the labour.

Nick brings me a cup of tea and a dish of prunes. When I am halfway through the bowl, the phone rings. It is Kypros.

'How are you?' he asks, gently. I know immediately that he knows all that has happened.

'I'm OK,' I told him. 'I'm sitting in bed eating prunes.'

'You must be pretty sore.'

'Yes, I am.'

'Well, you've been through a lot of hell and suffering and you've been extremely courageous. You should be proud of yourself. And you know that you did everything you could.'

'Thank you.' I am really touched.

'You have my home phone number don't you? Please call me any time if I can be of any help.'

As I put the phone down I ask Nick, 'How many consultants would phone at ten o'clock on a Sunday morning and tell you how courageous you have been?'

I can just about reach the bathroom, with help, though peeing burns my tear horribly. Leaning forward is better, I find. I am very grateful that Katrina stopped Sarah from stitching it though, or I would have had to go through that too, just when I had had enough pain. I put a few drops of calendula tincture in the bath, to help heal the wound, and lie there looking at my pubic hair, hidden from my sight for four months, and my floppy abdomen, no longer Glastonbury Tor, more like an empty sack. I cry, my tears running into the bath water. Relief that I won't have to go through any more physical pain or anxiety, relief that I know we did everything and there could have been no better outcome for Alice, alternates with the loss, the emptiness of having no baby to hold, and the broken connection with that little spirit, which kept me going for so long. I remember Tiggy, the cat we had when I was a child, wandering around the house mewing after her last kitten had been given away. I feel a deep down, unnameable gap.

I spend the day sleeping, talking to people on the phone, and crying. Each time I cry, Nick comes across from the studio where he is painting, and silently puts his arms around me, rocking me as I sob, 'My baby, my little baby.' I go over and over the whole birth and death in my mind, and then again to friends and family who phone. It is almost all I can talk about. We have been living on the edge of life and death for so long, and it has all ended too abruptly. I have to dwell in it, to relive all the varied emotions so that they will eventually release their hold on me. I go through the grief of her loss again and again, but I also start to be able to appreciate the triumph of giving birth naturally. I know that I might never have seen her alive if I had had a Caesarean and been unconscious.

I wake up to hear Nick on the phone, taking care of someone else who has called in, in shock and grief. We both find that in taking care of how other people feel, we also take care of ourselves. We need to talk about what happened, and other people want to hear about it. The people who have supported us, intending Alice to live, support us now in her death.

Looking in the mirror, I can see the deep dark rings around my eyes and my pale skin. I lost at least 15 litres of amniotic fluid, full of nutrients, and I have been through physical and emotional stress. But despite being so ill and sad, I am not plagued by depression or thoughts of 'Why me?' We have the chance to talk about Alice and the birth as much as we need to. But also, the homeopathic remedies which my homeopath sent (free of charge), and the healing from the New Forest may have contributed. I simply experience whatever is going on, and feel very alive. Nick feels the same, and we are drawn even closer by the whole experience. I hear later than nine out of 10 relationships break up after a cot death, and feel sad that so many people don't have this kind of support.

On Monday morning I want to go back to King's to see Alice's body, so we phone Nicky and Katrina, who arrange it and take us there. I manage to get dressed, putting on my needlecord pinafore over my still over-sized tummy, but can't walk more than a few steps. A wheelchair is found for me, and we follow the long corridor down to the mortuary. I don't know quite what to expect, but I am amazed to be taken into a little square room, with grey curtains drawn round all four walls. There is a little niche in one wall with two artificial candles burning. In the middle of the room is a Moses basket on a stand. Alice is lying there covered in a turquoise blanket, a red fabric rose laid across her chest. Most of the oedema has gone down, so you can see her face, though her eyes are shut fast, and her mouth is open, where the tube had been.

Nicky and Katrina leave us alone with her, and I lift her from the cot. For the first time I am aware of holding my baby, this tiny little human being that Nick and I made, and who I grew inside me for months. It feels unreal and bizarre. This is the only chance I have to know her, now she's dead, now she isn't actually here. I feel her tiny hands, with long artistic fingers like Nick's, and I examine her minute fingernails. She is cold, but still floppy, like a doll. Her hips seem to be locked into place, drawn up and slightly hunched over to one side. I feel her tiny feet and doll's toes. I stroke her silky, fine black hair and touch her little ears, soft as petals. I notice how my arms feel, holding my baby, and I realise that holding your own baby, even when dead, is completely unlike holding someone else's baby. But she isn't even my baby. This is just her body, and will soon start to decompose. I feel no horror at this. Love overcomes it all. I cry and feel this sad mixture of wonder and grief. I want to imprint this time on my mind.

Nick holds her for a while, then gets out his sketch pad and draws a little picture of her, lying in the cot. Nicky also mentioned the idea of taking hand- and footprints, so he has brought a little ink-pad, the kind for a rubber stamp. After a few unsuccessful attempts, Alice's palms and soles are rather black and we have a good set of prints. Each footprint is 6.5cm long. Then Nicky comes back and takes lots of photos. After a few hours, we decide it is time to move on. I borrow the camera, and take one photo of her profile, looking almost as if she is asleep in the basket. As Nicky pulls my wheelchair back out of the chapel, it is the last view I have of her. I burst into tears as we make our way back up the corridor.

As we cross the large hall, we see Ruth, who squats down beside me and holds my hand. I find, as I dry my tears, that I am so proud to be able to tell her how I'd given birth to Alice naturally, and how we'd seen her before she died. It would be so easy to see the experience as nothing but a complete waste – all that energy and pain for nothing. I feel everyone will expect it to be like that. But that isn't what it is like. We are determined not to sink into disappointment. Most people would have their child be their triumph. For us, the birth is our triumph. The opportunity both Nick and I have had to give more than we ever thought possible, to be heard, appreciated, and to have our wishes followed, have transformed it into something beautiful and pure as well as painful and sad, something full of joy as well as grief.

In the lift we bump into James Bernard, who looks a bit uncomfortable but says hello to us and asks me how I am. I reply that I am OK, and add, impishly, 'You see, I didn't need syntocinon after all!' I feel rather gleeful. I've got my own back now, so I can forgive him.

Next we go to see Diana Singh, whose job is to comfort and counsel parents of babies in the Neonatal Unit. She has a little room next to the Fred Stil ward, with plants on the shelves and bright pictures on the walls. She is kind and sympathetic. She gives us tea, in real china cups and saucers, various pamphlets from SANDS (The Stillbirth and Neonatal Death Society) and copies of the poems pinned to her noticeboard. When I read *When a Baby Dies*, full of people's accounts of their baby's death and how they coped afterwards, I am surprised at some of the stories. Many people have little support from family and friends, who misguidedly think that it is best not to talk about it, or are embarrassed to mention it. Many husbands can't handle their wife's grief, and don't know how to express their own. We are so lucky that we've spent years in an environment of open communication, and are surrounded by friends who are also willing to be open.

While we are talking to her, Bobby Gasper, the house doctor who looked after Alice, comes to see us. He gives us the medical certificate of her death, and I ask him more about what happened.

He says her lungs were much smaller than was thought from the scan; apparently it is difficult to judge capacity with the distortion of ultrasound pictures. They were giving her 100% oxygen, not mixed with any air, which meant her lungs were clearly not designed to work. We also discover that her heart almost stopped beating for six minutes when she was born, so even if it had been possible for her to live she might have been brain-damaged. I realise later that it must have been about six minutes from her birth to the moment when I leaned back and gave all my attention to her, talking to her in my head. I feel sure she had come back for me, to say goodbye properly, before leaving. When you have been so close to someone, have been their life source, have given everything for them, you notice things like that.

Finally, we go up to the Harris Birthright Centre. I try to walk down the corridor, because I don't want all those expectant mothers to see an exhausted, post-natal woman with black rings under her eyes being wheeled down the corridor. But I think being hardly able to walk is just as bad. Angela sees us and immediately forestalls the journey by showing us into the midwives' room, where we sit once more on the little blue sofa. We say we want a 'team photo', and please will she fetch Kypros. Then we sit down to wait for him. We show Alice's footprints and Nick's sketch to Ruth and Angela, then Douglas, when he comes in. I don't want it to end. This place, despite all the pain and fear I have been through, has become like another home to us.

Eventually Kypros sweeps in and squeezes himself on to the sofa next to us. We all smile for the camera, then I show him the footprints, the hand-prints and the sketch. He seems more interested in looking at them for signs of talipes and other symptoms of Arthrogryposis, than for their sentimental value, but I don't mind. Most people can show off their baby when it's born; the just reward for pregnancy and childbirth. All I have are a few small images, so I am determined to show them to people, the physical evidence that I too am a mother. The experience I've been through is invisible. I am desperate to communicate it. Then there is a pause and Kypros looks at me. He obviously wants to say something to remind us of the seven long weeks we have all spent together, but also to look forward to the future. So in true Kypros style, he pats my large empty tummy and says, 'Now you'd better get rid of this, or Nick will be going to The Olive Tree to find some other woman.'

The next day we discover all about cabbage leaves. I never realised before what medicinal properties the humble cabbage has. My body, of course, not realising my baby is dead, has set about preparing the colostrum and milk, the hormones being triggered off by the birth. And as the milk is not emptied out, my breasts start to get hot and swollen. By the third day, Tuesday, they are extremely hot and painful, so that I can't lie on either side, but have to lie on my back. Nick, following Nicky's suggestion, has bought a white cabbage. He tears off the outer leaves and puts them in the fridge. When they are chilled, he rolls them with a rolling pin. I put them inside my bra and feel the inflammation lessen. We have fun doing it, as it seems so absurd, but it is very effective. Not only does the coldness help, but cabbage actually contains some substance that reduces inflammation. Every two hours or so, I pull out the leaves. They are now warm and even crisp, and I call out for more.

My mother once told me when I was young that wet nurses were often people whose babies had died. The infant mortality rate in Manchester in the 1860s was 500 per 1,000 live births: for every two babies born, one never reached its first birthday. The stillbirth rate must have been similarly high, so many poor women who could well do with the money must have dragged themselves off their beds to find a middle-class mother who wanted a wet-nurse. I imagined them all, sitting feeding a baby that wasn't theirs, crying quietly for their own lost child.

It takes a week for my breasts to cool down. Either Nicky or Katrina visits me each day to check that I am healing properly, both physically and mentally, and Nick goes off to the Register Office. He brings back a birth certificate for Alice, and her death certificate. Here is the formal acknowledgement that she lived. I think of two friends whose babies were stillborn and therefore hadn't officially 'lived'. There is virtually nothing between their situation and mine, except they had the added grief of seeing their perfectly formed babies and thinking 'If only…' I am so grateful that Alice obviously couldn't have lived. It was strangely perfect.

I spent all those years at The Hunger Project speaking about the infant mortality rate of different countries, never dreaming that my daughter would become part of the IMR for Britain – 11, wasn't it? Out of every 1,000 babies born alive, 11 will die in their first year. Not because of the underlying cause of hunger, as in developing countries, but from various diseases and conditions. Fifty percent of these deaths, and stillbirths, are never explained, as Alice's never was. It was clear why she died. As to why she developed as she did, there was no explanation; the post-mortem was inconclusive.

Alice has given me a new way in to those faceless statistics. The numbers represent children, and for each one, some woman has been through the pain of childbirth, has loved their child dearly, and has mourned their death. I think of the faces of the women I passed in Nepal. How many of them had lost children? How many mothers did I not see because they had died in childbirth? Death is so invisible to the outside world. But I glimpsed it, once. At a tea stall I saw a young woman with her little bundle – a baby a few days old. She showed it to us shyly, her face glowing with pride and love, and we smiled back. But the baby was still, pale and peaky: the shadow of death hung over it, and she had no idea. When her baby died, would the shock make her grieve for her baby more than

I grieve for Alice? How can one compare such things?

There used to be pockets of female infanticide in certain villages in Tamil Nadu. A friend who had been to a village and spoken to women who had killed their baby girls, spoke of the dead and haunted look in their eyes. I can now get a glimpse of the horror they must have been feeling at what they had done, and the resignation. There was so much family and social pressure. My friend recalled their sad, hopeless justification: 'We don't want our daughters to have lives like ours.' No schooling, an arranged marriage, taken away from their home, worked hard and sometimes cruelly treated, often underfed and anaemic, forced to kill all daughters except, perhaps, the first. Their desperate, unfulfilling lives were in front of their eyes. Later, The Hunger Project ran a highly successful campaign to promote the status of women. Short advertisements were shown in every cinema featuring famous film stars with their daughters, and special social workers were trained in each village to make 'vulnerable' families aware of the services available for girls. Within a few years, the infanticide died out. The advertisements were then shown in every state in India. In terms of what The Hunger Project's campaign accomplished, that was just the tip of the iceberg. Who knows what other possibilities are opening up for Indian women as a result?

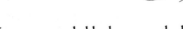

We are surrounded by beauty as the house fills up with bouquets of flowers and beautiful cards. We talk to my mother almost every day on the phone, but she also sends us a note. 'There seems so little I can do except offer admiration and sympathy but I keep thinking of you.' At the end she had added a PS: 'I expect the flat is full of flowers – get some more when they fade.' She has enclosed a cheque – typically kind and thoughtful. It reminds me that when I was travelling around India, often quite lonely, I could always count on my mother to write to me every week. Her letters were a lifeline; especially when other people hadn't written for a long time.

We also have an increasing stream of phone calls. It must take courage for each one of them to call. Their first words are tentative and sad, feeling their way across thin ice. They always relax when they find that we are willing to talk about everything. All those calls, all the conversations we have about Alice, make such a difference to us, and we can't help but see they are making a difference to other people too.

There are a few conversations that will be particularly ingrained on my memory. One is with Lillian, who is 72. She has a son aged 50, with teenage and adult children, and a daughter aged 40, who is pregnant with her first child. She is a lovely person, warm and understanding, full of life. She calls to say how sorry she is to hear about Alice, and I start to tell her how we went back to see her on Monday, how she was laid out in the Moses basket, and how we were able to hold her for as long as we wanted.

'Oh, if only it had been like that in my day,' she says.

'Yes, I was really lucky,' I tell her. 'They even help you wash and dress your baby after she's died, and give you a new clean dress.'

'I lost a baby, too, you know.'

'Really?' I am surprised. I know the family quite well, and this is news to me.

'Yes, it was when Howard was three, so it was just right that I was going to have another baby when Howard was small. I started to go into labour when I was at home, and my husband drove me to hospital. But when I got there I started to haemorrhage. My husband was waiting outside; you know, husbands didn't come in with you in those days. But he started to realise that something was wrong, as they were wheeling bottles of blood into the room, and so on, so he asked to come in and see me. They wouldn't let him. I must have been in a really bad way, because I can't remember much. I was losing a lot of blood. I nearly died. But I do remember clearly seeing a beautiful white light, and wanting to go towards it, and then I looked down and saw myself lying on the bed, and my husband was holding my hand. Somehow he had got into the room and was determined I would live. And so I pulled myself back. I can still remember how hard it was, but I knew I had to stay for him.'

I am just listening, rapt by this story.

'And when I came around,' she continues with difficulty, 'they told me my baby had died and I had to give birth.'

'Oh, no!' My heart goes out to her. 'That must have been so hard, to have the grief and the labour all at once.'

'But, Chrissy, the worst bit was that when he was born, they took him away from me. They wouldn't let me see him. I was screaming 'Give me my baby!' but they said 'Just forget about it. You can have another one.'

She is crying.

'It took me years to get over it. I couldn't understand why God had let this happen. And you know, it wasn't till long after I'd had Deborah, and I began to see how special she is, that I realised that I would never have had her if my other son had lived. Because I only ever wanted two children.'

I understand from Lillian's granddaughter that she has never spoken about this time before, and now she starts talking about it with her family. A few weeks after this conversation, I receive a card from Lillian. On the front, inside a border of coloured flowers, there is a poem:

'Then shall I know...
Not till the loom is silent
And the shuttles cease to fly,
Shall God unroll the canvas
And explain the reason why
The dark threads are as needful
In the weaver's skilful hand
As the threads of gold and silver

In the pattern He has planned.'

A few days later I hear that Lillian has died. She went to dinner with her whole family: her two children and her three grandchildren. She was happy. She went home and died in her sleep. And though I am very sad and shocked, I can't think of a more perfect way to die, complete and contented.

⟋

Sara, as always, is supportive. She never stops relating to me as a mother, and later buys me a copy of The Body Shop's *Mamatoto* book. I am on the phone to her, telling her all about Alice's birth, and how at least I avoided a Caesarean and pushed her out myself. She sighs and says, 'You know, I still feel I failed with Emil's birth. It still gets me after all this time.'

'Failed?' I ask. 'What happened? You had to go to hospital didn't you?'

'Yes. It all started off nicely at home, but it took so long. And after about 10 hours I felt I just couldn't take any more. I wasn't dilating fast enough and I was getting so tired out. So I gave in and they took me to Guy's. They gave me an epidural, so I didn't feel anything, and I never really felt I pushed him out.' She starts to cry. 'I always feel, looking back, that I could have kept going, and I missed out on something. I'd had this whole picture, as well, of giving birth at home, with candles, and a hot bath, and, you know what it's like in hospital: bright lights, all clinical and sterile. And even though we took Emil home that day, it wasn't the same. I didn't give him the entry into the world I'd wanted.'

I know exactly how she feels, and she knows exactly how I feel. How would an outsider understand that I, my baby dead, can feel a satisfaction about the birth that was missed by someone whose baby is alive? But perhaps only mothers will ever understand it – I don't know.

In between phone calls I write letters to thank people at King's. I still need to be doing things connected with Alice, and my time at the hospital. I write to Kypros and the team at the Harris Birthright Centre, to Diana Singh, Bobby Gasper and Dr Gamsu. And I write to Sarah Creighton. I realise in writing to her how lucky I am that she delivered my baby and not James Bernard. Though he is probably perfectly competent, I didn't feel comfortable with him. This is what I write to Sarah:

'Dear Sarah,

You made my experience of giving birth to Alice so perfect and special that I wanted to let you know just how much it meant to me.

From every doctor I came into contact with – Dr Stott and the others on the labour ward, I experienced a thoughtfulness and deep concern to do the very best for both Alice and me. Given there were so many unknowns concerning Alice's condition, I felt they all, and Dr Gamsu, gave me their carefully considered judgement on the best course of action.

But when I looked into my own integrity, I knew that Alice's condition couldn't be looked at as a set of probabilities; I had to give Alice every possible chance, and for me that meant a natural birth, despite her being breech. You recognised the strength of my commitment and something that every woman knows – that the pain of childbirth lasts for hours, but the pain of even the smallest regret can last forever.

You balanced your trust in me with sound good judgement at every stage, you explained everything to me in a way that left me totally trusting you, and you delivered my baby with gentleness, consideration and skill. My two-and-a-half hour second stage was hellish, as my over-stretched uterus had given up and I had no urge to push at all. But the faith you had in me, and Nicky and

Katrina's knowledge of me, allowed me to experience the triumph of pushing Alice out, a triumph that will strengthen me for years to come, long after the sediment of pain has settled and is forgotten.

The fact that I had no Caesarean enabled me to spend that precious half-hour with Alice while she was alive, and feel her hold my finger. Having no episiotomy meant I could go home that night to recover from my state of shock and exhaustion, and was well enough to come back and spend time with her little body on Monday when much of her oedema had gone.

My picture of hospitals has been irrevocably altered out of this experience. I was aware of the love and support of all the midwives, particularly Jan, Elise and Katy, and all the other staff I met, and I also experienced being listened to, empowered and treated with dignity.

Seven weeks ago I dreaded going to King's – now it feels like home.

Please show this letter to everyone involved and pass on my deepest thanks to all the staff.'

I feel much better when I've written this, and when I see her a little while later she tells me she has never had such an appreciative letter in her whole career.

We receive so many cards and letters – all of which I keep in the gold box Nick gave me for Christmas, which just becomes known as 'Alice's box' – and the few from the hospital staff make me realise how rarely they are thanked. I have seen thank you cards up in hospital wards, but they are generally to the nurses, and not the doctors. Maybe people feel more at ease with the nurses, and would not dare to write and thank a doctor. Or maybe they do write, but a doctor wouldn't put a letter up on the notice-board. Kate Jackson, the head of midwifery, who I only met once, but who gave Nicky and Katrina honorary contracts so they could be my midwives in the hospital, writes to us:

'It is hard to adequately express my admiration for the way in

which you dealt with the stress and grief that you must have felt as
the seriousness of Alice's condition became apparent to you. Your
consideration of others at that difficult time was an inspiration to
everyone who was involved in your care. I am so sorry that Alice's
life was so short.'

I have always been a manic list-maker, so I indulge in this harmless
habit to prolong the experience of my time with Alice. I list all
the fortuitous moments in the history of Alice's birth and death,
all the people who phone us and who send us letters, cards and
flowers. I make three alphabetical lists: of the people we met, the
people to invite to the funeral, and the medical terms we have
learnt. Alice lived and died in this hospital; it was her whole world
and community. It has a fascination for me.

We spend a long time planning the funeral. I track down an
old friend, John Cullen, who is a minister and used to teach with
me. He agrees to lead the service. We all discuss ideas till we are
clear we have designed it exactly as we want. Some people want a
small, quiet funeral when their baby dies, but we want to thank
all the people who have supported us. So many people have been
through this experience with us, especially the last seven weeks of
waiting and wondering, that we need something to complete it
for everyone.

It is two weeks till I am strong enough even to go to the funeral
directors by taxi, so we schedule the funeral for February 15th and
send out about 100 invitations. I know you don't usually send
invitations to a funeral, but it seems appropriate. We know these
people will want to be invited. Alice's short life and death will not
be hidden away. None of my small family is able to come, except
my aunt from Woking, but a few of Nick's family are expected,
and lots of friends. We send an invitation to Kypros, Douglas,
Angela and Ruth.

Kypros sends a reply thanking us for the invitation and for the donations to the Harris Birthright Centre that family and friends have sent in. It doesn't actually say whether he is going to come, so I phone Angela and she says she'll ask him.

'But do you know, darling, he has never been to a funeral in his life. Grateful parents are always inviting him, but he never goes. He's frightened of being upset, I think. You know how he takes it to heart so much when one of his babies dies.'

'Yes, I do. But think how much grief he has stored up. And he's only ever experiencing people's distress. He hasn't had a chance to feel how a funeral can give you a sense of healing and peace.'

'You're right; he hasn't.'

'Will you make sure he comes? After all, it's on a Saturday; he's got no excuse.'

'OK, darling, I'll try my best. But I can't make any promises. I'll be there, anyway.'

I have to leave it at that.

Chapter Nine

Transformation

He who binds to himself the joy
Doth the winged life destroy;
He who kisses the joy as it flies
Lives in eternity's sunrise.
                    William Blake

By the morning of the funeral, I am calm. I have been over it again and again in my mind. I am prepared. The doorbell rings and here are Isabel Knight and John Holland on the doorstep, hugging us, tears mingling with smiles.

'You two are so inspiring,' says John, gazing at us with tears in his eyes, holding our hands.

'Chrissy, you look so calm,' says Isabel.

Nick and I sit in the back of the black limousine, holding hands, and staring at the tiny white satin-covered coffin in front of us. One of the undertakers drives the car at a snail's pace while the other walks slowly and formally in front. We realise it is to gather our huge cortège, (which consisted solely of John's sports car, Nick's brother's car and his aunt's car) but it passes through both our minds that maybe he is going to walk all the way. Soon both undertakers are in their car, and we stop briefly at the florist's to pick up the little bunch of white flowers we've ordered to put on Alice's coffin. We anxiously look at our watches as ten-thirty looms nearer, but there is nothing to be done. It feels good, the formality and ceremony, the sense of being taken care of, and driving in such a beautiful car. It seems almost bad to admit that I am actually enjoying this part. What a contrast to my father's funeral, where the agony of my grief seemed to fill my whole world. I wonder how many people notice the size of the coffin as we drive past the crowds of Saturday shoppers.

We turn into the cemetery and stop for a moment at the lodge. As the driver goes in to report our arrival, I look with curiosity at the car in front of us, which has also stopped. We know ours is the only funeral today, so we wonder which of our friends is ten minutes late. As they drive forward we see it is Kypros and Angela, both smoking heavily.

At the top of the hill, we stop on the large sweep of tarmac, and through the huge open doors of the chapel we can see the backs of our friends and family, 60 of them, standing waiting, the winter sun streaming on to a rich blue carpet in the central aisle. Kypros and Angela are just walking in, to take a seat near the front. On the doorstep, John Cullen welcomes us with a hug, and then we walk slowly up the aisle, following the undertaker carrying the small white coffin on his shoulder. Our old friend Eugene is playing the organ, and everyone is still. We sit on the right, at the front, and I am aware of everyone's attention on us, our little family.

John speaks of how I contacted him and told him that I'd had a baby, and that, as he opened his mouth to congratulate me, I had gone on to tell him that she had died. He speaks about the juxtaposition of birth and death, of the joy and the sorrow, balanced in this whole experience.

I look at the little white coffin, lying on the huge dais. I look at the three steps leading up to it, the blue carpet, and rows of bouquets laid out below the pulpit. I take in everything, soak it up to go over and over it in my mind afterwards.

John finishes speaking, and sits down. I hear Isabel's footsteps coming up the aisle and watch her walk up the steps. She turns to face the congregation and reads.

'Footprints.'

I glance down at the Order of Service in my hand. It just has 'Alice 18.1.92' on the front with the prints of her tiny feet underneath.

'One night I had a dream. I dreamed I was walking along the

beach with God and across the sky flashed scenes from my life. For each scene I noticed two sets of footprints in the sand; one belonged to me and the other to God.

'When the last scene of my life flashed before us I looked back at the footprints in the sand. I noticed that at times along the path of life there was only one set of footprints. I also noticed that it happened at the very lowest and saddest times of my life. This really bothered me and I questioned God about it.

' "God, You said that once I decided to follow You, You would walk with me all the way but I noticed that during the most troublesome time in my life there is only one set of footprints. I don't understand why in times when I needed You most, You would leave me."

'God replied, "My precious, precious child, I love you and I would never, never leave you during your times of trials and suffering. When you see only one set of footprints it was then that I carried you."'

I remember the surprise and the tears that had sprung in my eyes when I first heard that piece. The surprise has gone, but I still love it.

As we sing *Lord of all Hopefulness* I hear Nick's voice, and the voices of all the people behind us. My heart swells with love and pride as I think about how they are singing for our baby. We won't be able to bring her to parties in a baby-carrier amid admiring exclamations; we won't be able to see her smile, and watch her take her first steps. We will never be able to take her for a walk in the park, nor have birthday parties for her. We will never hear her talk or watch her making friends. Yet she has made friends, and they are here expressing their love for her and appreciating the difference she has made to them.

Next Sara, Rosa's mother, and John Holland, give two readings from Kahil Gibran's *The Prophet*. We have chosen them carefully to express something of the value of our experience. Sara begins:

When love beckons to you, follow him,

Though his ways are hard and steep.

And when his wings enfold you yield to him.

Though the sword hidden among his pinions may wound you.

And when he speaks to you believe in him,

Though his voice may shatter your dreams as the north wind lays waste the garden.

For even as love crowns you so shall he crucify you. Even as he is for your growth so is he for your pruning.

Even as he ascends to your height and caresses your tenderest branches that quiver in the sun,

So shall he descend to your roots and shake them in their clinging to the earth.

Like sheaves of corn he gathers you unto himself.

He threshes you to make you naked

He sifts you to free you from your husks.

He grinds you to whiteness.

He kneads you till you are pliant;

And then he assigns you to his sacred fire, that you may become sacred bread for God's sacred feast.

All these things shall love do unto you that you may know the secrets of your heart, and in that knowledge become a fragment of Life's heart.

But if in your fear you would seek only love's peace and love's pleasure,

Then it is better that you cover your nakedness and pass out of love's threshing-floor,

Into the senseless world where you shall laugh, but not all of your laughter, and weep, but not all of your tears.'

John continues with the theme of joy and sorrow:

'Your joy is your sorrow unmasked.

And the selfsame well from which your laughter rises was oftentimes filled with your tears.

And how else can it be?

The deeper that sorrow carves into your being, the more joy you can contain.

Is not the cup that holds your wine the very cup that was burned in the potter's oven?

And is not the lute that soothes your spirit the very wood that was hollowed with knives?

When you are joyous, look deep into your heart and you shall find it is only that which has given you sorrow that is giving you joy.

When you are sorrowful, look again in your heart, and you shall see that in truth you are weeping for that which has been your delight.'

I know that around the room are all our dearest friends. Rachel and Lynne are each taping the service, Joe has given out the Order of Service sheets, and now Sarah is coming to the front to sing. She stands by the organ, smiles at me as Eugene plays the opening bars of Bach's first prelude, and then sings *Ave Maria* over it, a lovely arrangement by Gounod. It feels as if the beauty of every note vibrates through me. It is almost a physical anguish for the exquisite nature of this song and the whole ceremony. In the following days I will play that song on the tape over and over again, and it will never lose its almost magical nature.

Then Nick stands up, and walks to the front, with two pieces of paper in his hand. For a while he just looks down, preparing himself to read.

'This is a letter to Alice, from me,' he begins, and his voice is slightly broken with tears. He swallows and continues,

'Dear Alice,

This is a mystery to me, who you are, where you come from. We seem to have been living on the edge of life for months. My grandmother died recently and in the years before she died it was as if she was a child again, living in the small world of an old people's home, looking after her companions and offering to make tea for visitors. When I think of her, I think of that old young person of 91 or alternatively of the person in a photograph I'd seen of her as an open, bright-eyed young girl of about 12.'

A picture flashes before me of his grandmother's funeral, and the family gathering afterwards, where I sat on the sofa, roundly pregnant and proud of my burgeoning motherhood.

'I never saw your eyes or heard your voice,' he continues, 'but I want to speak to you as a mature human being, as mature as any of us. In your brief life you have asked for nothing, seen nothing, made no demands. Your life has been one of pure contribution. To your mother and me you have given a new sense of love and intimacy and closeness.'

It is strange to hear him say that phrase, 'To your mother and me'. It is the first and last time he can say it to Alice, and I wonder when he will be able to say it again.

'To me you have given yet another opportunity to grow up, to be responsible for my life. And to many of us you have given the possibility of making an extraordinary experience out of the worst possible circumstances.' I can hear various quiet sniffs around the room, the surreptitious taking out of handkerchiefs.

'We live our long lives slowly perfecting ourselves – maybe you are so perfect you needed to live only a few short hours. This is a mystery to me, who you are, where you come from. But I do know that you will always be with us and we will always be with you.

All my love, your father, Nick.'

I feel such a love for him, I'm so proud of him, and the rawness of my grief is bathed by the sense of love I experience for both of us, really for all three of us, from everyone there. I keep my eyes fixed on him as he starts, in a slightly stronger voice, on my letter.

'My darling Alice,

'I know that time and time again I will go through that terrible, painful beauty of missing you, of longing to hold you, and yet I am at peace. I know that grief, like birth, has its own pattern.

My life will never be the same again now. Not because of what I have lost, but because of the enormity of everything you have given me. How glad I am that I had that last 45 days to appreciate you and live my life out of my love for you. In that period I discovered strength I never knew I had. Each time I mastered one pain or anxiety, there was another one to confront, like carefully graded lessons in the expression of love. But I would have gone through much more for you, for now I know the extraordinary, unfathomable depth of a mother's love for her child, and its power and passion leave my life so much richer, so much deeper.

'And what a bond we formed! You sent me such beautiful, peaceful messages and gently prepared me by telling me you were ready to die. You could so easily have given up earlier, or faltered in that long labour, but you even stayed long enough for me to say all that there is to say; long enough to hold my finger, hear my voice and slip away.

'But your spirit is still here – for yours was not a private life, and nor is your death. I have experienced such love, support, such joy and friendship from so many people because of your existence. I know that you have touched and altered the lives of people all around us, sending ripples into the world. What you have left me with, you beautiful, strong little soul, is a more intense, ever-present joy in life and its mystery, a much deeper love for people and an even stronger passion to live my life to the full, as you lived your brief life to the full.

'You will always be my daughter, and I will always be your mother – nothing can change that now. And I am glad. I wouldn't have it be any other way.

'With all my love, your mother, Chrissy.'

I see Kypros wipe the back of his hand across his eyes, as Nick sits down, and I hear people crying quietly. Time will move on, but this moment when people are moved is recorded for posterity on a small cassette tape. John ends with some prayers, and, as he tells everyone how the service will continue at the graveside, I go through a tearful moment, realising that this is it; the little white coffin that I have stared at for half an hour will soon disappear forever. Nick holds my hand as the undertaker hoists it on his shoulder again and we turn and follow him down the aisle, across the windy tarmac and into the car. We watch our friends pour out of the door and find their cars to follow us down the hill.

The grave looks tiny, deeper than it is long, and everyone forms a large silent circle round it. As we trickle our handfuls of earth onto her coffin, I feel the sadness of letting go, but I am also glad that Alice, and the experience of our loss, lives in a small way in all these people. We are not alone. When the prayers finish, the silence continues, and everyone just stands, the cold February wind whipping around them. Eventually Nick and I turn and go back to the car, to be driven up to the hotel.

When I first walk into the room we have booked, I see that they have given us both rooms, not just one. They have joined the oak-panelled room to the white one, and laid out all the little tables with white cloths and pink napkins. The sun is streaming in at the bay windows, and John and Isabel have put flowers on each table. It is difficult to believe it is February; there is an air of spring filling the place. Tea, coffee and biscuits are served as everyone comes in, and each person hugs us, hugs each other and seems to glow with light in that beautiful room. There is something extraordinary in the atmosphere. It seems so pure, so loving; the balance of joy and sorrow seems to have transformed itself into this room full of love and gentleness.

After a while we get everyone's attention and speak, thanking all the people who have helped us and supported us, through the weeks of waiting, the birth, the death, the funeral. There are so many people who have helped. Finally we thank Nicky and Katrina, our two partners up the mountain, who made so much possible. Then our friends start to say things; how the experience has inspired them, how wonderful it is that death can be talked about like this, what great parents we are. One friend says, 'It seems strange, but this seems the best possible place to be today. I couldn't think of a more wonderful place to be than here.'

And this is how it is. As we walk out of the hotel, a full moon is shining palely in the clear blue sky.

Postscript

A couple of years later, to my delight and amazement, I saw a 10-minute programme about Vanita on BBC2's *Rainbow Reports*. I remembered how I had seen her last, sad and smartly dressed in her best sari, standing outside her house near Amari Mandali to be photographed. Her husband was with his new wife in another village. I hardly recognised the woman I saw on TV. It was 10 years since I had seen her but she looked 10 years younger. Her hair was tied back, but loosely, she was wearing a salwar-chemise, and looked confident and alive. She had trained as a health worker, and travelled around, re-teaching the women about the traditional remedies they could make from the plants in the forest. She enabled them to see the importance of the forest to their lives, in an area increasingly threatened by deforestation. We watched her getting on a bus in Songadh, remarking how she didn't like the town: it was dirty and full of fumes. She preferred the peace and cool of the forest. We saw her on the verandah of a house, showing a group of women how to make a paste that would cure scabies. The women were chatting and laughing; she looked so happy and fulfilled.

She had been given an opportunity, and with it she had transformed her life.

Appendix 1

The Hunger Project

'You would be mistaken if you thought of The Hunger Project as just another NGO. The Hunger Project is a movement, a network of hundreds of organisations and individuals committed to the creation of a new human being.'

Dr V.S. Vias, Chair, Institute of Development Studies, Jaipur, India

I cannot do justice to the power, effectiveness and ever-growing impact of this extraordinary organisation in this brief summary. I highly recommend a visit to its web-site at www.thp.org. I include this appendix to give you some background to the references to The Hunger Project in Chapter Five, in the time of the first era, (mentioned below) and how this connects with the very different work now going on.

The Hunger Project is an unconventional, strategic organisation. It does not provide 'relief', or show people what to do. Rather, it works in authentic partnership with the people of developing countries to address the root causes of hunger and to ensure that all people have the chance to lead healthy and productive lives. Working in 13 countries in Africa, South Asia and Latin America, it carries out proven strategies that are empowering millions of people to achieve lasting progress in health, education, nutrition and family income.

In addition to directly empowering hungry people, The Hunger Project works strategically to change policies, catalyse society-wide transformation of the conditions holding hunger in place, and strengthen the local democratic structures through which people can meet their needs on a sustainable basis.

'Gender equality is more than a goal in itself. It is a pre-condition for meeting the challenge of reducing poverty, promoting sustainable development and building good governance.'

Kofi Annan, Former United Nations Secretary General

The highest priority in all The Hunger Project's activities is the empowerment of women. The greatest obstacle to ending hunger is the severe subjugation, marginalisation and disempowerment of women in many developing countries. Society holds women responsible for all the key actions to end hunger: family nutrition, health, education, food production and – increasingly – family income. Yet, through laws, customs and traditions, women are systematically denied the resources, information and freedom of action they need to carry out their responsibilities.

In the first era of The Hunger Project's work – from 1977 to1990 – one critically missing element for the end of hunger was a global commitment to this goal. The Hunger Project carried out a massive campaign to make "the end of the persistence of hunger by the end of the century an idea whose time has come." It was its intention to make the issue clear, finite and urgent and to call forth the global commitment to bring hunger to an end.

That campaign succeeded. In September 1990, at the largest gathering ever then held of international leaders – the World Summit for Children – this goal became the commitment of the world. World leaders committed themselves to a series of goals which, if fulfilled, would have meant the end of the persistence of hunger by the year 2000.

Once the commitment existed, it was clear that the world lacked the strategies and approaches that would enable it to fulfil this commitment. This launched the second era of The Hunger Project's work – the era of fulfilment.

While the world has not yet fulfilled its commitment, enormous progress has been made. In addition, the world has gained a fundamentally different understanding of what needs to be done to achieve the "final milestone" for the end of hunger. Catalysing this action is now the focus of The Hunger Project's work.

Appendix 2

Landmark Education

"Landmark Education is an international leader in the training and development industry. It offers programmes that are innovative, relevant and immediately effective. These programmes challenge conventional perspectives and decision-making patterns, and provide new tools for effecting significant change – shifting the very nature of what is possible. As a result, participants can see new possibilities for effective action, achieve higher standards of excellence, and act beyond existing limits.

"The Landmark Forum is specifically designed to bring about positive and permanent shifts in the quality of your life. These shifts are the direct cause of a new and unique kind of freedom and power: the freedom to be absolutely at ease no matter where you are, who you're with, or what the circumstance; and the power to be in action effectively in those areas that are important to you. In independent research, Landmark graduates report major results in the following areas:

- *The quality of their relationships*
- *The confidence with which they conduct their lives*
- *The level of their personal productivity*
- *The experience of the difference they make*
- *The degree to which they enjoy their lives*

Fun, exciting, collaborative, The Landmark Forum is not a lecture, motivational technique, or therapy – it's a powerful, accelerated learning experience."

Extracts from Landmark Education brochure

For more information, visit www.landmarkeducation.com

I want to acknowledge the difference Landmark Education has made to the whole experience of our time with Alice. I have highlighted a few here:

• The relationship between Nick and myself: clear, open communication and intimacy.
• Being able to listen to thoughts as thoughts, not fixed truths; to distinguish our thoughts from what was actually happening.
• Creating a powerful context or project, enabling us to be the authors of our lives.
• Choice: to choose what was happening rather than being at the effect of it.
• A large support network of people; being able to talk freely about our experience.

Appendix 3

Useful Organisations

Antenatal Results and Choices
   73 Charlotte Street. London W1T 4PN
   020 7631 0280
   Helpline M-F 10am-5.30pm 020 7631 0285
   www.arc-uk.org
The only national charity which provides non-directive support and information to parents throughout the antenatal testing process.

Association for Improvements in Maternity Services (AIMS)
   5 Ann's Court. Grove Road. Surbiton. Surrey KT6 4BE
   Tel: 0870 765 1453
   Helpline: 0870 765 1433
   www.aims.org.uk
Campaigns for better understanding of the normal birth process and also provides support and information about maternity choices.

Association of Radical Midwives.
   www.radmid.demon.co.uk
UK midwives who are committed to improving maternity care within the NHS – a support group for midwives and for women who cannot find the care they need.

Babyloss Support Group
   PO Box 1168. Southampton SO15 8XZ
   email: support@babyloss.com
   www.babyloss.com
A resource of information and support for bereaved parents and their families who have lost a baby at any stage of pregnancy, at birth, or due to neonatal death..

BLISS
2nd & 3rd Floors. 9 Holyrood Street.
London Bridge. London SE1 2EL
Tel: 020 7378 1122
Parent Support Helpline: Freephone 0500 618140 10am-5pm
email: information@bliss.org.uk
www.bliss.org.uk
The premature baby charity. Practical and emotional support for parents whose babies need intensive care or special support.

Cruse Bereavement Care
Cruse House. 126 Sheen Road
Richmond. Surrey. TW9 1UR
Tel: 020 8939 9530
Helpline: 0870 167 1677
Young person's helpline: 0808 808 1677
www.crusebereavementcare.org.uk
National charity set up to offer free, confidential help to bereaved people. They produce booklets which you can buy on-line.

Foundation for the Study of Infant Deaths (FSID)
Artillery House. 11-19 Artillery Row
London SW1P 1RZ
Tel: 020 7222 8001
email: fsid@sids.org.uk
Helpline 020 7233 2090   M-F 9am-11pm, w/e 6pm-11pm
www.sids.org.uk
Support and information service for parents and families who have suffered a cot death.

Harris Birthright Centre for Foetal Medicine
King's College Hospital. Denmark Hill
London SE5 9RS
Tel: 020 7924 0894

Infertility Network
  Charter House. 43 St Leonard's Road
  Bexhill on Sea. East Sussex TN40 1JA
  Tel: 08701 188088
  www.infertilitynetworkuk.com
National charity providing advice, information and especially support for people suffering from infertility, sub-fertility or with an interest in fertility. Also includes 'More to Life': a support network for the involuntarily childless.

The Miscarriage Association
  C/o Clayton Hospital
  Northgate. Wakefield
  West Yorkshire WF1 3JS
  Tel: 01924 200795
  www.miscarriageassociation.org.uk
Provides support and information for those suffering the effects of pregnancy loss.

Stillbirth & Neonatal Death Society (SANDS)
  28 Portland Place. London W1
  Tel: 020 7436 7940
  Helpline 020 7436 5881 M-F 10am-4pm
  www.uk-sands.org
SANDS provides a nationwide network of support groups for bereaved parents and families, and campaigns for improvements in care during pregnancy and when a baby has died.